Stories from The Farm In Lucy

THE GRACES
WE REMEMBER

Sacred Days of Ordinary Time

PHYLLIS TICKLE

LOYOLAPRESS.

CHICAGO

LOYOLAPRESS.

3441 N. ASHLAND AVENUE
CHICAGO, ILLINOIS 60657
(800) 621-1008
WWW.LOYOLABOOKS.ORG

All Scripture quotations are from the King James Version of the Bible.

"Of Bulls and Angels" first appeared in *Homewords: A Book of Tennessee Writers* (Knoxville, Tenn.: Tennessee Arts Commission and University of Tennessee Press, 1986) and is used with permission of the publisher.

"To My Pear Trees" and "Haying" first appeared, in slightly different forms, in *The City Essays* (Memphis, Tenn.: Dixie Flyer Press, 1981) and are used with permission of the publisher.

Cover and interior design by Megan Duffy Rostan
Cover photo © Bill Boch/FoodPix/Getty Images

Library of Congress Cataloging-in-Publication Data
Tickle, Phyllis.
    The graces we remember : sacred days of Ordinary Time / Phyllis Tickle.— 1st Loyola Press ed.
        p. cm.
    ISBN 0-8294-1767-2
    1. Pentecost Season—Meditations. 2. Fasts and feasts—Christianity—Meditations. 3. Farm life—Religious aspects—Christianity—Meditations. 4. Tickle, Phyllis. I. Title.
BV61.T52 2004
242'.38—dc22

2003019969

Printed in the United States of America
04 05 06 07 08 09 10 11 M-V 10 9 8 7 6 5 4 3 2 1

Contents

Prologue

Homemade stories, my late mother-in-law used to say, are really just facts that people own in much the same way that they own any other part of their household goods, all of which are a little overvalued, a little ragtag around the edges, and a little antique in form. Once was the time I acknowledged Mamaw's observations as folksy, if not downright quaint. Now that I am as old as she was then, I know better. Folksy and quaint or not, her analysis is certainly true. (There is, of course, a lovely irony in my having discovered no readier way to open a book of homemade stories than with the tale of a matriarch's insightfulness. My matriarch would probably have regarded this as more curious than quaint, however, for she was a staunch realist who brooked no romanticism and little self-indulgence.)

This, then, is a collection of facts that have been owned down into stories, Lenten and Easter stories that are more accurate, perhaps, and more possessed now than they were even when I first wrote them. I say this because, by the grace of God, the young lives—mine and Sam's as much as our children's, children-in-law's, and first grandson's—whose progress is captured here in still-frame have gone on to mature in the ways of the heart, the body, and the land. In our growing we have carried these spring tales with us, most of us to places other than the farm, but each of us has continued to catalog and edit them as one does a library of heritage and identity.

In 1976, when our country was celebrating America's position of wealth and world dominance almost as much as—perhaps even more than—it was celebrating the hardtack independence that had been our founding, Sam and I finally found the courage to confess to each other what we both had known for several years. Both of us had been born late in our respective parents' lives. Both of us, as a result, had been reared by a generation whose youth had been spent more in fields and barns than in groceries and dry goods stores; and also as a result, both of us had been taught by unspoken and unselfconscious, albeit exquisite, daily example how to grow and tend, make and make do.

What he and I confessed to each other in the autumn of 1976, then, was that not only did our children have none of these skills, but they also possessed none of the freedom or the discipline that come from knowing how to live with and on the land. Ultimately, it is always the land and what it knows that sustain life; and it was to the land that we had to take them before it was too late. So with five of our seven children still at home, we began to look for what Sam described to the realtor as "adequate acreage and a solid barn with a useable house somewhere on it." That phrase probably said it all, for the next year we signed the paperwork on The Farm In Lucy without his ever having been inside the useable house. It was sufficient to his way of thinking that the barn was incontestably solid and that the pastures would sustain at least two-dozen head of cattle.

Lucy, Tennessee, if you should ever chance to come here in person, is only about twenty miles due north of Memphis, Tennessee, and twelve or thirteen miles, as the crow flies, from the eastern banks of the Mississippi. In 1977 it was also separated from Memphis by at least a hundred years. A town that had devolved into a village that, by the time of our coming, had devolved into a community, Lucy had once been a thriving stop on the Illinois Central Railroad. As Memphis had grown, however, the pull of commerce had shifted south, leaving Lucy as a quiet little village with a couple of general stores, a fine old school, and about four thousand citizens if, as we used to say in town meetings, one counted the tractors as well as the cows and people.

The pull now, of course, is in the opposite direction; and as the city spreads closer and closer, the number of people goes up as the number of tractors and cows goes down. Thus even now we still number about four thousand in aggregate, but we count ourselves in souls these days rather than resident entities. We have only one general store on Main Street, though it is by common agreement the best we've ever had; and we still have the state's most accommodating old country schoolhouse, despite the fact that it suffered the insult a couple of years ago of a totally utilitarian addition on its back side. The community church whose bell, in our early years, tolled the village's dead as well as our worship, is now a wedding chapel that tolls nothing, for its steeple and bell have long since been removed.

In all of this change, Sam and I have changed as well, of course. The Farm In Lucy—as our children and their children call it now, complete with capital letters—The Farm In Lucy is hardly a farm these days except in memory. No herd grazes here, no horses are stabled here, no crops grow, and this year no garden was even planted. Common sense would say that we are too old to want the responsibility of such, and common sense would probably be right; but more to the point, common sense also says there is no need any longer. The lessons have been taught, the gifts given, the children reared. What the land teaches has passed on to them. That part of it is done.

Sam and I spend a good deal of time these days praying that the children and their children and, now, their children's children will keep the faith. But as surely as the original writing down of these stories was a way to forestall any forgetting, the retelling of them here has been, for me, part of this new way of praying. And in the certain knowledge that family prayer is best said in community, I hope you and yours will join me and mine in this one. The latchstring is out on the door at The Farm In Lucy.

CHAPTER 1

About Garbage and Redemption

You have to understand about country garbage to understand about that particular St. Barnabas Day.

It was one of those clear, light, almost-not-there days when everything is easy because there are no boundaries, no divisions in the world. The inside was as cool and as warm as the outside. All the doors were open and all the windows raised, but it wouldn't have mattered if they hadn't been. The freshness would have found us anyway, traveling as it was on slides of sunlight through everything. School was out, and there were no schedules to keep. The children's freedom was still recent enough so that it was not yet a burden to them or to me. A golden day set in the middle of a golden week.

Holy days, when they fall during the week, are usually observed at midmorning and at eventide in the country, so celebrating St. Barnabas at ten o'clock was our first and only obligation beyond enjoyment this day, except for taking the garbage to the dump; and that, too, is a kind of enjoyment for me—an adventure.

John had loaded the barrels into the truck the night before and put the tarp over them, lashing the whole with his own very solid brand of roping so that the tarp wouldn't flap and tear. We were definitely a truckload of country garbage on the way to the dump, but we were going to be a neat load of country garbage, nonetheless.

When we first came to the farm to live, we used a dump that was no more than a quarter of a mile down the highway from our church. So long as that dump was active, it was a common sight on non-Sunday holy days to see several pickup trucks loaded with garbage barrels in the church parking lot during midmorning services. Much to our private regret, however, the dump filled up after a few years, and we were then forced to go five miles farther north past the church to a new landfill. It was every bit as interesting as the old one, of course, just farther away for us and nearer for most of our fellow parishioners. The most obvious result of this shift in the scheme of things was that now our fellow worshipers didn't bring their garbage to church; we still did.

Now if there's anything in the world that upsets a fifteen year old, it's being different. And being different, like everything else, has its gradations, the agony of each adolescent being in direct proportion to the remarkable degree of his or her differentness. Thus, by the time we were the only communicants routinely hauling our truckload of refuse to holy days, John had developed a genuine reluctance toward both religion and trash. And because I strongly believe that adolescent boys are better haulers and toters of fifty-gallon drums than are their mothers, he and I were not infrequently at loggerheads about why we were taking the garbage yet again and about why he was going with me when we did it. His strong protests that I had done it alone when he was little and that I would have to do it again as soon as he and Sam Jr. were grown were entirely irrelevant to the parent in charge, namely, me.

So he grumbled and I honestly cajoled (I was not totally insensitive to his position). Then came the fateful morning of St. Barnabas's feast, 1985, when John, Becca, and Sam Jr. trooped out to the truck. Trying to wedge myself into the cab with them, I realized that our days of disposing of garbage this way were indeed being numbered by their growing bulk, but I was not about to say so, much less give John the satisfaction of any hope just yet. So, grateful to the core that this was an easy holy day, I cranked us up and away we went to St. Barnabas.

The service that morning was remarkably unremarkable. Barnabas has been a favorite of mine ever since someone told me, years ago when I was a child, the story of his missionary trip to Lycaonia. The Lycaonians were so taken with his good looks and handsome physique that they thought he was Jupiter, king of the gods. In fact, so the story goes, they almost sacrificed a cow and some incense to him before he managed to stop them. That image—that palpable sensation of being even briefly seen as godlike and worthy of sacrificial homage—so moved my childish ego that I have loved old Barnabas ever since. As an adult I have certainly been curious about what kind of grace makes a Barnabas tick.

The homily that morning, just as on every other St. Barnabas Day of my life, had been full of religion and contained none of the poetry of having a face and a body that look like they belong to the king of the gods. It was an awful shame, I thought, and the observances had been, as a result, also an awful shame.

When we came out of church forty-five minutes later, the world had warmed up a bit. In fact it was hot, and the cab had downright overheated under the mid-morning sun. We climbed into our forced intimacy, and windows rolled down, wind blowing, and tarp holding, we hit the highway and the fifty-five-mile-an-hour ride to the dump. Much as I love air-conditioned cars, the joy of near racing just doesn't happen without that extra stimulus of wind and grit in my face. The needle of the speedometer went to sixty and was approaching sixty-five when Rebecca said, "Mama!" Sometimes I thought that she was the oldest and most staid child in the world. No romance of the open road and all of that in the child at all. But I did slow us back down. The barrels and Becca sighed with relief, and the boys grinned. They at least could always be counted on to enjoy the race to the dump.

The man who ran the new dump was a dour sort of fellow. One had to have a rather particular kind of worldview to run a dump, I imagined, and I enjoyed eliciting his from time to time. You did not have conversations with this man, of course. He didn't have that many words per customer in his daily allotment, but he was always good for a brief—one or two sentences maximum—assessment of you or your garbage and/or that of the driver and truck that just left.

Of all the semiconversations we had had in our three years of speaking to each other, and of all the situations I had seen him rise to, two—both dramatic, to say the least—stick in mind as indicative of the man. The first is the time I saw him unexpectedly draw a pistol out of his shirt and take the head off a rat twenty yards away. "Ain't been no rats in this dump so far and ain't ever going to be" was his one-sentence summation of that event. Sure enough, I've not seen another rat since then, although I still think a pistol a rather extreme, if not expensive, solution to the problem; but a man who takes pride in his work is entitled, I suppose, to his own choice of methods.

My second commanding memory is of the day some poor soul backed too near to the edge of the dump shelf and slid right in—truck, barrels, and all. It took the bulldozer and a dozen of us onlookers to pull the fellow out. "Shoulda left the durned fool down there if he's that blind" was the overseer's summation on that one. "Downright dangerous to have folks like that on the roads these days . . . 'sides, he smells to holy heaven now."

And leaving the bulldozer's huge motor idling, he was gone to direct another pickup into place on the shelf.

It was not unusual on a warm and slow day for him to come and greet us, which he did that morning. He then usually stood and watched wordlessly while the boys dumped the barrels, which he also was doing that morning. One barrel dumped, Sam moved the second forward, and John tilted it over. Sam moved the third to the tailgate, and John bent to tilt it.

"'Scuse me, lady, but I think you've throwed away your cat."

His tone was so laconic, so matter-of-factly factual, that neither the boys nor I reacted at first. John tipped the third barrel as if nothing had been said, and then just as he tilted the load beyond recall, we all three registered what we had just been told. There, beneath John's cascade of falling garbage, was Alouette, scrambling up through rotten peels, soggy rags, and old cans, one kitten still dangling drunkenly from her mouth.

I hollered. John hollered. Sam Jr. hollered. John jumped off the tailgate, Sam vaulted over the side of the truck, and I took off running. Alouette made it halfway down the shelf before we caught her. The kitten, not more than twelve hours old, was frantic by the time John got it separated from Alouette's jaws and began to cuddle it. Alouette, for her part, fought me every step of the way back up to the truck, turning and slapping at me as we climbed. I held her at arm's length and hollered at Becca to close the cab windows and get ready to receive one mad cat. John put the kitten on the floor at Becca's feet, and I set Alouette on top of it, slamming the door as fast as I could behind her.

Then we started sorting the piles we had just made, following the mewing as it led us to kitten after kitten. Each time we unburied one, we beat on the cab for Becca to crack a window enough for us to hand in another kitten. It was not until we had found and reclaimed all six of them that Alouette was more or less content to stay unrestrained in the cab with Becca. By that time all four of us were dripping with sweat and dust, the boys and me from clambering through garbage and from exertion, and Rebecca from being shut up in the steaming cab with the cat family.

The boys made fast work of the remaining barrels, except one we left half full so that Alouette and her family could be reinstalled as soon as we got back home with them and their nursery of choice. We rolled up the tarp and lashed the empty barrels in. Becca held Alouette's nape while the boys and I crawled back into the cab. Through the closed window, I waved our thanks to the overseer still standing there propped against his dozer. He raised his hand, and through the glass I heard him say, "Bye, lady. See you next time." Then, "Better make them boys take a bath, though. They smell to holy heaven." Beside me John died yet another adolescent death, and wise old Rebecca said, "It may stink in here, but at least you won't go so fast with the windows up."

Suddenly I started laughing. In less than one hour's time we had gone from Mass to this, and the contrast was just too much for me. I had an image of Barnabas with his body like the king of the gods looking down at us so newly and so odorously come from his commemorative day. What a chuckle he must have gotten out of this holy day . . . and what a chuckle he must have gotten out of his own first "holy" day! To have some benighted soul come up and try to lay a heifer open, guts and all, at your feet must—like sorting garbage to retrieve kittens—tend to put lots of things in perspective for one, and rather quickly, too. It certainly would give one a sense of humor about the human condition.

And that was what the sermons had never said in all those years. Barnabas had had a sense of humor. He must have. It was the only thing that made any sense. I sobered at that epiphany.

"Hey, kids, would you mind if I named one of the kittens Barnabas?"

They didn't. Of course they didn't know why either, but they let me do it anyway. Before long he was sitting out there on the patio watching me, grooming his thick fur, holding court for me through the window, reminding me that sometimes, as a special grace, we still can find a part of our soul's salvation wrapped in the gift of laughter.

CHAPTER 2

Peter, Paul, and Granny

The real reason we live in the country is that there is no longer a city anywhere that would ever let us store and house all the material goods Sam requires in order to feel secure and complete in this life. Not only is the man a keeper and a saver, he is also a worrier. He is the kind who is absolutely sure that someday a cataclysm will come and we will be caught without everything that, had we been morally responsible, we would have stockpiled in order to survive it.

During the Cuban missile crisis I had the only cellar in the state of South Carolina that could have sustained life for a full year for a family of five, including the requisite supply of bottled water, string, pins, needles, garbage bags, razor blades, pencils, and so on that such a year would require. As a matter of fact, we could have lived more comfortably in the cellar that year than we did upstairs.

But now, more than forty years later, all that the intervening years have done is to increase the clutter and to hone Sam's habits to a pitch of consummate perfection. We now have everything and can face any eventuality—except that of running out of space to store it all.

When we came here to the farm years ago, there were only a barn and one outbuilding for storage. The barn looked immense to me, and I sighed a sigh of release from both anxiety and embarrassment; we would never fill it up (want to bet?) and no one could see us while we tried.

In all honesty I have to admit that the barn was vacant when we moved. Six weeks later, however, with a full herd and their supplies installed, the barn was considerably less impressive. Nonetheless, since we were coming from a normal city house on a normal city lot (one we had stretched to its fullest potential), the barn effectively absorbed all of the things that had so compromised me in the city.

You see, what Sam Sr. acquires and/or saves really is necessary rather than elegant. Years ago, for instance, he had torn down a back wall on our lot in the city; had carefully cleaned each of the bricks as he tore the thing down; and had carefully hauled each of those same bricks to the country with us when we moved: "A man can't ever tell when he will need a good brick or two." Now, there's nothing wrong with that position as such, and there's nothing wrong with having a brick pile handy behind the barn, but there had been, and always will be, a great deal wrong with having a brick pile in a city yard.

The same may also be said for a collection of thirty-two one-gallon mayonnaise jars which may indeed be a great help someday. I haven't the faintest idea for what, but for something no doubt, especially since the man who gave them to Sam was, I was told, married to a spendthrift who simply could not see their potential and was being quite unreasonable about their presence in her city garage. They went quite nicely into the back stall of the barn and, for all I know, still sit there awaiting their day of purpose.

The string-to-rope collection of everything that could ever be used to secure anything filled up the entire corridor wall in the new barn; but it looked so much better there than it had in our city bedroom, kitchen, laundry room, and den that I was overjoyed that first summer to walk through a corridor of cinctures every time I visited the cows. Likewise with the lengths of pipe, all of varying diameters, which, laid flat across the rafters, now constituted the ceiling for two paddocks of the barn—a solution infinitely better than having them propped on end randomly around the backyard fence in town.

In fact, one of my most portentous memories is of driving with Sam, one afternoon before we moved, through heavy city traffic. He pulled into an intersection and stopped for the light. Then, with an "Oh, my goodness!" he opened his door, leaned out into the street, and struggled to retrieve what turned out to be a length of pipe about two-and-a-half feet long and a half-inch in diameter. He was jubilant as he landed it successfully into the backseat before the light changed. It was typical of our relationship that I hadn't even seen the thing and that he chatted happily all the way home about how good it was to have yet another length of scrap conduit around the place. It was shortly after that that I began to actively campaign for a move to the country.

Before a decade had gone by, the barn had suffered certain additions—about forty feet protruding from its former front and another forty protruding from its former back. It was a little hard to distinguish exactly where the old barn had been, and it was a much longer walk than it had been to get anything out of the string-to-rope collection.

There was also a rather ungainly wooden thing near the barn. It was a bit too large to be a shed and a bit too awful to be a house, but we filled it to its roofline with good stuff, all of it very good, in fact. We compromised our aesthetic differences, Sam and I, by painting the whole thing a flat, dull green that rather faded into the landscape for at least eight or nine months of the year.

The hen house, always an active place, was also reengineered to allow for considerable storage. The hens originally seemed to share something of my point of view about any changes in their environment, but they proved to be equally ineffectual in getting things their way. So now they just lived on resignedly with the gallon cans, the scraps of sheet metal, and the chipped pottery that might someday be needed to start seedlings in.

The newest old structure was a compost house, or at least that's what it was when we came here. Before long we had roofed it and sealed it up to become a weather-tight storage area for the lawn tractor, the bicycles, the hand mower, the hand tools, and the twenty-two shelves that came out of the old village store and would some-day prove invaluable. The windows out of the store would not, I regret to say, fit in the revamped compost house, so they were propped outside against the back wall until we could figure where to build some structure or other in which they would once more be functional.

Now all of this I could tolerate in my husband because, first, there is some truth in the assertion that country living, unlike city living, really does require a considerable supply of ready-to-hand debris with which to patch and fix. We were too far out to get service reps to fix—either reasonably or quickly—most of what went wrong; and we were much too far out to drive in for materials every time Sam had to fix whatever it was that did go wrong.

In the second place, and equally true, I knew before I got him that he was this way. His first cousin, in fact, never married because, by his own admission, he never could find a woman who would let him keep his plow on the front porch. So it's not as if I can say that I didn't know going in to this arrangement that he was one of those in whose hands frugality becomes a vice.

And third, I suppose I must admit to a certain weakening on my part. It was nice to be able to get two bricks every time I wanted to protect a plant or prop up a flowerpot. It was junky, but also handy, a compromise I never could have imagined in myself back in those city years. How I, with all my years of fretting and protesting, could now have a place above the freezer for storing all the tinfoil pie plates that came in from the store was beyond me. I found it downright alarming, moreover, that I had a sizable section of the shop dedicated to storing various boxes and shipping containers that, who knows, I might need any day for mailing something somewhere or for packing away something or for loading something into the car or a million other such possibilities.

But even allowing for my softening as well as for my foreknowledge, the truth still is that our life together as a household has been one long exercise in what my mother, while she was still alive and living with us, used to call robbing Peter to pay Paul. What she meant by this favorite aphorism was always a mystery to the children when she would mutter it under her breath with a shake of her head or utter it to me as a logical device for family discussion. And they would ask repeatedly what Grandma had against Peter and which Peter was she talking about anyhow?

Applied to our cause, of course, she simply meant that given Sam's compulsion for always being prepared, we have always needed increasing space in which to store the "essentials." The list of essentials has always increased, of course, in direct proportion to the expanding facilities and space that had to be maintained so that we might store the required essentials with which to maintain the expanding space, et cetera, et cetera. It is a pattern that, as each child matured, he or she came to recognize more clearly in us and accept more charitably. Each also came to appreciate more completely the utility of Granny's pet aphorism, so that even twelve-year-old Rebecca could apply it quite accurately to the appropriate situations.

One afternoon she came in from her chores and asked me what happened when Peter was robbed dry and Paul was too full to take on more. Since I was in the middle of a serious casserole and my mind was on ovens rather than philosophy, I did a double take. *What in the world was she talking about?*

"Well," she said, "since the barn goes all the way to the edge of the pasture hillock in back now and all the way to the garden gate in front and since we've run out of sheds and the compost house is full, I just wonder what Daddy was going to do about Peter and Paul."

Before I could even think my way into the intricacies of her metaphor, I heard John behind me say, "Same as God did with the originals: pass it all on to us." He was propped against the hall door, just as he was at the same time every night, waiting for his dinner and indifferent to every concern except food.

"Yeah," said Becca as she set the fresh eggs into the sink and began to wash them, "then you better be sure you're as good a man as the originals."

For my part I was glad to be occupied with the casserole, strongly suspecting as I re-covered it that there was little that I or anyone else should add to the conversation.

CHAPTER 3

To My Pear Trees

After my bath I stay long in the tub, listening to the soft, cotton suck of the water as it circles the drain. I lie through that instant of near bursting when my bones take up the weight of my flesh again from the retreating water. I feel the vacuum as it pulls my back hard against the porcelain bottom and as flat as if I were young again. My skin and hair release the water, droplet by droplet, to the gravity of air and drain, and I live briefly in the slow effervescence of their drying.

Even when it's finally gone, this will still be my water. It will come back again to me, to my body, to our house. It leaves now in copper pipes which run off into cool clay ones which, in turn, drain just beyond the orchard fence into the gravel overrun where, purified, it sinks slowly under the roots of grass, trees, and vines.

Some spring soon it will flower or make milk for a
new calf; some fall soon it will drop from the juice of
our pears or fatten a steer for market. This water leaves
us only for a few seasons.

In its origin it is not our water, of course. City water
was brought into this part of the country years ago,
brought without the consent of those who farm here,
brought in the name of the public good, and paid for by
assessment of the unwilling. Our house, like the others
in the community, had always been plumbed into its own
well. When the water came, each well, ours included,
had to be disconnected—severed from itself—and the
houses reconnected to pipes whose names no one knew.
In our homes water had become a manufactured necessity, a commodity to be produced elsewhere and trans-
ported at great expense to a dependent market.

The outside water was different. The water in the
barn, the water in the hen house, the water in the hose
pipes . . . that was our water . . . ours from our well and
brought up by our pump. The houses may have had to
be connected to utility pipes, but not the farms themselves. On the days when the utility company had the
water shut off to repair the lines or even on the days
when the pressure in the inside faucets was low, we

could still trip the pump switch and draw up what was ours, what was not another's to shut off or treat or pollute. It was an independence that even the younger children, despite their hatred of summer watering chores, fiercely valued.

Like me, they remembered the hot days in past summers when the well went out; when we watched anxiously as their father climbed up and down, up and down, from the ground to the well-house roof, rigging a homemade derrick; when in that devastating heat of 105 degrees, he pulled the well-shaft by hand, inch after inch, until it stood a hundred feet above us like a prayer tower into the belly of heaven. They remembered, too, the afternoon when, a new valve in place, he sank the shaft back into the water table; how we all stood waiting in the heat while he primed and primed and the water came racing out to the frantic fields and thirsty garden; how I cried when we saw it come; how he slapped the children on the backs; how we had an early supper and an early bedtime; and how the water sang all night in the hose pipes.

It was not long after that that the machines came. They were a mile or so away from us, near the village; parked for a day or two, growing in number until there were seven of them—backhoes and Cats and two flatbeds of concrete pipe. On Thursday of the last week of September the stacks of ten-inch pipe were dropped, a dozen pipes per strapped bundle set out every thirty or forty feet along the roadside. On Saturday the crews came and began the digging. Backhoes along the edges of the road, backhoes into yards, backhoes crisscrossing the roadbed. It was suddenly two miles to get around them, two extra miles around the crisscrossing to the school and community center, two extra miles to the market where we sold our eggs. Sewers were coming! Once more, without having been asked or even told, we stood helplessly as the heavy equipment lumbered across the land. The water we now had to pay to have hauled in was about to be wasted, hauled away, and we would have to pay for that, too. Our water was soon to pass totally through and beneath us in a sealed system of delivery as if it were a product and not a given.

The rains of October came, and the machines bogged down in the mud. We rejoiced when the great crustaceans were hauled away. All winter we hoped they would not come back to work the ditches. Of course they did, but times were hard, and there were fewer men, fewer machines. Only a dozen houses or so lost their last hold on the cycle of nature that had, since the beginning, nurtured them. As the fall ended and the winter began to move in, the machines were taken early to storage. They will come again next month or the one after that; eventually they will get us like they have gotten everyone else. So I lie long in this tub, feeling the water leave and sending it with love to my pear trees. How else, in what other way, can one mourn for the death of water, if indeed it is the water that is dying?

CHAPTER 4

A Promise Kept

July 22 is the feast day of St. Mary Magdalene. Of all the women in holy writ, she is the most difficult to correctly assess and, therefore, to accurately honor. She has long been labeled a prostitute, although the proof for that theory has always been wanting, and in recent years the scholars have doubted it more often and more publicly. Mary is scarcely traceable, for we know nothing of her lineage and almost nothing of her ending. But during the time of Christ's adult life, she was ubiquitous. From his earliest friendships to his resurrection scenes, there is Mary Magdalene. And that leads us to the question of *why*.

Why has been answered in at least two dozen different ways by literally hundreds of scholars over the centuries. Some of the answers are so sloppy and romantic as to be offensive as well as unworthy of the issue. Some of them are so shot through with theological burdens as to be intellectually effete as well as untenable. I think we do better by the Magdalene and her Lord if we take his word for it that only the sick have need of a doctor. That is, I think they were probably just friends, friends both because she was a sinner and because he was God.

Almost without fail, the company of people like the Magdalene is restorative and healing. Because they don't apply the rules to themselves, they have a wonderful tendency not to apply them to others. The resulting generosity of their viewpoint and of their conduct can refresh more deeply than any medicine I have ever taken.

It was to Mary, the all-accepting and the all-giving, then, that I think Christ must have turned frequently for human reinforcement. I imagine her having the kind of grace and openness of life that I will never have and that I truly envy—a capacity for contact and nurturing that we all would do well to consider if we, too, would keep company with her Christ. I came to this conclusion not from any Bible study, but from experience.

I have known two Magdalenes in my lifetime—known them well and openly, that is. Probably even loved one of them, to the extent that our diverse schedules could grant any real existence to our affection. Any knowledge of this world is a bit of a fluke, I suspect, for a middle-class woman like me with a houseful of children and more acceptable obligations. But apparently it was the writer side of me, and not the middle-class part, that each of them let in; the never-quite-fits-its-context side that each found paradoxical enough to accept.

Briefly, one of them—Vanna—even accepted me enough to participate, albeit distantly, in my family, at least to acknowledge that I had one and to come once or twice to supper or a birthday party. But that was hard for her. Awkward. The kind of awkward that finally becomes indomitable, and we slipped back into the easier business of being together, just the two of us, in the daylight hours of our lives. We had met originally at a writers' conference, for she sometimes still tried to support herself with freelance reporting. But eventually, because there was no real reason for us to see each other routinely, the differences in our lives began to erode our conversations and, in the end, our friendship.

But it was not like that with Bonnie. I can't even remember now exactly how it was with Bonnie, but I can remember how it started, and how it ended. It was years ago. Sam and I were still living in the city, still struggling to build careers as well as children, and Grandma had just come to live with us that spring.

Bonnie was a beautician in some little hole-in-the-wall salon that had just opened. I wandered in one day because it was there and I was tired. My hair is irascible in heat. It kinks up, knots, flies, refuses to style, and generally burdens me with an awareness that it is there. Because it's that kind of hair, however, and nothing is going to make it look unobtrusive anyway, I can enjoy the luxury of a walk-in shampoo anytime I'm feeling the need for self-indulgence, and I was feeling it a lot that summer.

Walk in and walk out. The original drip-dry, she called it that hot summer afternoon. That may have been what caught my attention. She certainly wasn't slick or posh or even ambitious as a beautician. That was probably what I understood first. She may have been the new owner of a small salon, but this wasn't her career, not really. I could sense it in everything about her. The minute she touched my head, the minute those fingers began to move through my hair, I knew that whatever she really did or really was, she liked giving pleasure. She had that rare gift of knowing enough about her own body to understand someone else's—and the rare generosity that allowed her to give away her sensuality just as casually as she had received it.

I went back after that, time and again, even when it meant driving a city mile or two out of my way. I went for the joy of the shampoo certainly, and because the enigma that Bonnie was kept drawing me in, though to this day I have no memory at all of what we talked about during those early shampoos.

Certainly the oddity that was Bonnie soon gave way to the oddity that was her shop. She was the only beautician who was ever there, and I was the only regular customer who was ever there. There were three stations, but over the months of that first summer they showed less and less evidence of ever being used.

On my sixth or seventh visit I came to understand that Bonnie must be living there, upstairs over the shop, and that she had two or three other women up there with her. They would come down sometimes, always in cheap cotton wrappers, a cigarette in one hand and a crumpled half pack in the other, to buy a Coke out of the machine in the back or to ask Bonnie for some change. Occasionally I would see a masculine shadow lounging behind one of them or a hand reach out to take the Coke that had been bought, but never did I see any of the upstairs people face-to-face. They simply waited in the curtained dusk of the supply room until Bonnie could attend to them.

There was, however, a swarthy, slender man—Carl, he said—whom she called her business manager and who was always cleaning the sinks or counting money at the third station. The relationship between them did not seem to be that of pimp and property, although there was no doubt in my mind by then that Bonnie was first and foremost a hooker, if not by popular demand, at least by instinct and preference.

I think it took me that long to understand because of Bonnie herself. She was clearly middle-aged. Her hair was carefully and artfully dyed, but nothing was ever going to make her body look under fifty again. I don't think it really bothered her that much, though. Certainly by the time we parted company three years later she had let her hair go gray. It gave her face a kind of softness that matched her body's, a kind of sweet quiet or ease with herself that was contagious.

Over the months of the next fall and winter, my visits became more regular, more a habit I depended on even if my hair didn't. I came; we talked; she restored my soul and called it washing my hair. Sometimes I brought her things from my kitchen, usually sweets that Grandma had made and sent her. Grandma had become Bonnie's second and only other regular shampoo customer.

One of my most delightful memories of my mother, in fact, is the day she came home and, black eyes big as coat buttons, said, "Do you know that I honestly think Bonnie is . . . is not supporting herself on that shop . . ."

"Is hooking?" I offered.

"Yes! Exactly. That's what I mean. I really do!"

But I noticed that the revelation of Bonnie's true calling never stopped my mother from going twice a week for a wash and set. Even more important, I thought, was the fact that it never stopped the flow of goodies from our kitchen to Bonnie's shop.

By this time, Bonnie had become very candid about the nature of her business, and we had long conversations about the evils that attended her profession, the human damage—the realities, I suppose they might be called.

Bonnie was equally candid about the nature of her relationship with Grandma and with me. She needed us. "It dresses up the shop to have you in here, and especially a nice old lady like Mrs. Alexander . . . makes us look legit, like a real salon," she said.

I shared this explanation with Grandma, and thereafter she took an almost criminal pleasure in fulfilling her obligation to Bonnie by speaking with elaborate sweetness and impeccable propriety to the patrol officer who had begun to stroll in to the shop far too frequently for Bonnie's comfort. Nothing so animated my mother's afternoon as a disgustingly prim conversation with Officer Tolliver about the weather, politics, and the desperate state of urban crime. Her role as defender of the interesting, if not the innocent, was one that she was still proud of long after Bonnie had closed the shop and moved Carl back to Illinois so they could be near his children.

Bonnie's relationship with Carl was a simple one, not at all what I had at first imagined for them. She had been a cook on the river—signing on to a boat going downriver to New Orleans; getting off and working awhile, as she put it. Signing on to another tug to push the barges back upriver, when she needed a rest, as she also put it. Although, she said frequently, there was little rest for a woman alone, cooking like that for an eight-man crew on a floating tin can. "Those boys!" She would shake her head in mock despair. "I swear I just loved 'em all!" Then, with great pride in herself, she would tell me, "I can still go down there to the dock right now and sign on with any captain on that river. He'd take me in a minute. Knows I'd be good to his boys. If it weren't for Carl, I'd do it, too."

Carl was her reason for being. She had made of him the surrogate life that many single folks make of their pets. Carl had worked the boats for years, and they had met there, had become friends there. But Carl had developed bad lungs. And they were getting worse. It was Carl's lungs that had driven him to Bonnie. It was Carl's lungs that had driven them both ashore. And it was Carl's lungs that were destined to take them home finally to Illinois for him to die.

"What will you do?" I asked her once, after they had decided to close the "business" and just before they left.

"Probably just live on with his boy and his wife. They've got a nice house up there, and they say I'd be welcome. I can draw Social Security off my wages from the boats in two more years. I can make it till then."

The last time I was with Bonnie, as she combed out my hair and began to dry it with the towel, she said, "You can do something for me."

It was unlike her to express her private needs or desires at all, and I understood immediately that moving

inland and north was not quite as easy a thing as she had
wanted me to believe.

"What?"

"You can write me into one of your books someday."

"All right, I will. But why? Why would you care
about that?"

"I guess I'm getting old," she said, "soft in the
squash, but it would make the whole thing seem more
like it's been worth it if somebody knew I'd been here."

"A lot of people know you've been here!" I was
appalled by the irony of it.

"Yeah, but in all these years I guess I never did anything for Bonnie. I never had time or else I just forgot
to. I wish now I had . . ." She stumbled. ". . . had built
something," she said finally, ". . . you know, or written
something, like you or even had a family."

"No, you don't. You would have hated being tied
down when you were younger, being rooted to a washing machine or a man."

She thought about it a minute or two while she tow-
eled. "Yeah, I would've, wouldn't I!" She grinned at me
in the mirror. Then, slyly, ducking her eyes, "Just like
you would've hated my boys." She combed on for a
minute. "God's crazy, you know that?"

"Probably, but why'd you say so?"

"He made all the rules and then made people like me who couldn't any more keep 'em than we could fly to heaven by ourselves."

"I always sort of thought that was true of all of us."

"I reckon so," she said, cheerful again. "Sure is why I hanker after him anyway."

As a confession of faith, it was as brief as it was unorthodox, but I never heard one I thought was more validated by the life and history of its confessor.

Three days later, as they loaded Carl's car with what they wanted to keep, I went by to say goodbye. As she hugged me, Bonnie said into my ear, so Carl wouldn't hear, "I guess I do make a family now with Carl and his kids, but don't forget about the book. I'd still like to be in a book."

I told her I would remember, and obviously, I have. But after all these years I don't want to leave it just as a promise kept. I want to say here, as I never could then, that Bonnie did build something even if she didn't know it and I wasn't generous enough to tell her so. I want to say that only in Bonnie and in one very simple country priest have I ever found the unencumbered humility that would let me or any other spiritual stray rest effortlessly in its faith.

So, Bonnie, forgive me if you are reading this. I have kept my promise, but the book I have put you in is not about you after all. It's about grace and about how I would to God that I had more of yours.

CHAPTER 5

Just a Little about Lawrence

We have a presence at our house. Even after all these years, Sam still does not like for me to broadcast the fact, so I don't make my statement casually or without reason.

His name is Lawrence, and he has been with us for forty-some years and two houses. When Nora was seven, Mary five, Laura two, and before John, Wade, Sam Jr., and Rebecca even were, we bought a house in the city. It was one of those circa 1900 houses that are always found in center cities nowadays. Originally a middle-class triumph, it and all the other houses around it had done a slow slide into disrepute. The surrounding houses had been refurbished and were ready to be recycled, this time into middle-class triumphs of inner-city restoration. Only this house stood between the neighborhood and possible perfection.

With three young children, a college teaching appointment, and a doctor-husband returning to school for a fellowship in pulmonary medicine, I could muster almost no enthusiasm for house restoration, much less whole neighborhoods of it. A quick rundown of family finances, however, militated for the present, dilapidated choice. The house we had been renting was to be condemned for an interstate exchange, a fate I thought was eminently appropriate considering the eccentricities of both its plumbing and its heating. It was not that I hated being evicted, but that I despaired of what we were being evicted to. Nonetheless, as Sam so succinctly put it, this house was all there was. Take it or leave it.

We made an offer on the house, one slightly in excess of insanity and even more in excess of what we could afford. Obviously Sam had decided that he was going to solve the fixing-up problem by leaving us no money at all with which to fix up. It was at least one way to get out of the work for which neither of us had time nor energy. So he made his offer, I held my breath, and the realtor laughed out loud. The owner would never take it, no way ever! She already had refused three other offers that were considerably higher. The last one had been only four thousand dollars more, granted, but it had been from her bishop himself, who had wanted to put a boys' home there. The realtor elaborated in detail what a major decision it had been for her; and since— devout Roman Catholic that her late husband had been and that she still was—she had not succumbed to the pull of church and clergy, he felt it was very unlikely that she would succumb to us in our evicted state of need. Sam shrugged—I remember the gesture well— and said it was the best we could do; ask her.

That night, sitting morosely in our about-to-be-demolished kitchen, we got a phone call. It was the owner herself calling to say that she had received our offer and was accepting it. Never one to dally with the niceties, I heard myself responding with a simple "Why?" To which she responded, "Because Lawrence told me to. He wants a family in the house." It never occurred to me to ask her who Lawrence was. In fact, so great was my state of shock that I didn't even question what she had said until days later.

So that fall we moved—bags, baggage, and babies— into a house that had been empty for several years and that we more than casually distressed in all its seams and crevices. We cleaned and ripped out and made do as best we could, for there truly was no slush fund for repairs and restoration. Over the weeks that followed we met all the neighbors, warm, energetic folk with whom we were to share the next sixteen years and—naturally, was there ever any question?—the restoration of the neighborhood. Yet none of them was named Lawrence.

Once we were settled, or as settled as we were going to get without any money, I became friends with the former owner just by sheer contact and numerous phone calls about how we made what work and when. Finally one day during our first Christmas holidays in the house, I asked the question: "Who is Lawrence?"

She laughed the most cascading, musical laughter I can ever remember hearing. It was crystal and happy and almost angelic, so much so that it startled me, for Rose, much as I liked her, was neither crystalline nor cascading. Lawrence had been her husband. He had died in the upstairs front bedroom. He was still there. Hadn't we seen him yet? He was very happy that we had come. He had, in fact, been the reason she hadn't sold to the other bidders. Lawrence was very opinionated about people, even in this life, and he had become more so in his new one. We'd see him soon, she assured us.

Sam listened to my recitation of our conversation and then shook his head. "Crazy," he said, a position from which he has moved only grudgingly and with deliberation over the years since then. He threw in an addendum. "Doesn't the Roman Catholic Church allow some of this angel and ghost stuff into its credo?" We were young, you see, very young, and we had not yet met Lawrence.

It was not long, however, before we began to understand Lawrence. Mary, age five and chubby with a kind of Mediterranean beauty, was sleeping in Lawrence's bedroom. She had chosen it as hers before Rose's explanations, and she had no intention of leaving it now. She thought a ghost was "a pretty neat thing" and a dead man's bedroom was "even neater," to quote her. (She was young also, a child of our own infancy.)

Then came the spring and Mary's complaints that Laura was pulling the covers off her bed during the night.

"I don't think that Laura can get out of her crib," I insisted.

"Then it's Nora," Mary countered. "Somebody is yanking my covers off and waking me up!"

"Have you ever seen either of them in your room?"

No, she was always sound asleep when her "bratty sisters" came in. Finally, after numerous mornings of complaint and equally insistent denial on the part of the two accused, I suggested to her that we secretly set her clock for three-thirty, since four o'clock seemed to be the hour of her harassment. Maybe, if she could wake up in time, she could catch the culprit red-handed. She thought it was a marvelous idea—also neat, I believe—and I set the clock for her. Nothing happened.

"You told them I was going to try to catch them!" she accused.

"No," I said, telling the truth. "No one knows we set your clock."

We tried again. Nothing. By the fourth night she was getting bored with the game and also cross from interrupted sleep. I suggested that we give it up, but she was adamant. She was going to keep on until she caught one or the other of them. As I looked at her sleep-deprived eyes, it occurred to me for the first time to wonder why the errant sister, whichever one she was, did not look equally haggard. Surely if nighttime pranks could weary one child, they should weary another equally as much. Curious.

Then on the fifth night, Mary came bursting into our bedroom without knocking, a strictly forbidden violation of house rules. "Mother! Mother!" She was inarticulate. I had to see right now. I staggered into her bedroom (after three babies, Sam had learned to sleep through anything), and there was her bed, disheveled, the covers torn loose at the foot.

"He opened my door and came in! I saw him! He's doing it! Look!" And as I looked, her rocking chair began to rock merrily. Then it stopped just as abruptly. "Isn't it wonderful!" She was ecstatic.

Poltergeist? I didn't think so. It was much too benign, and the rocking of the chair had been jolly, good-humored, almost avuncular. I decided to say nothing. Children, unfortunately, have no such sense of decorum. The breakfast table was abuzz next morning with ghosts and nocturnal miracles, to which Sam contributed a withering "Humbug!" for the children and an "I want a word with you" for me. The drift of his thinking was that we were in no way going to encourage this kind of thing. It was patently impossible and not at all funny. Having no answer, I beat a discreet retreat from the field of battle.

Lawrence, however, did not see it that way. He continued to wake Mary, but she became adept at going back to sleep. Also, as the weather grew warmer, the air on her feet became less of a chilling shock, and she managed to sleep soundly through the summer months.

Then the other girls began to see Lawrence in the hall, a phenomenon that both Sam and I credited to active imaginations and to a certain amount of jealousy of Mary's honored role as harassee of choice. That is, until I saw him. He crossed the hall one afternoon from the bedroom toward the upstairs front bath just as I was mounting the back stairs. He had on a darkish overcoat with the collar pulled up counterspy-style and a brimmed hat pulled down so that I could see none of his face. I could also see through him to the wallpaper pattern beyond, an unexpected attribution that I found rather disconcerting.

Having heard well my husband's admonitions and having agreed (whether he would believe that or not) with his position that enough foolishness was enough, I had not engaged the girls in any detailed conversations about Lawrence since the spring. That afternoon, however, I broke the silence. "Nora, what does Lawrence look like?"

"I don't know. You can't ever see his face. He's got this hat on all the time, pulled down like. And some kind of overcoat-like thing with the collar up."

"Can you see through him?"

"Oh, Mama! Of course you can! You don't think he's really there, do you?"

I suddenly felt cold inside and, at the same time, intellectually piqued by the contradiction in my child's statement. "Then where is he?"

"How would I know? He just likes us and likes to play with us."

I left it alone, but I never forgot it.

In the dining room of the house there was a most remarkable chandelier. It was so remarkable that my father—a very godly man of much learning and most gentlemanly ways—when he first walked into the dining room, looked at it squarely and said quietly, "That's the most God-abandoned thing I've ever seen!" It was the only time in my whole life I heard him use that expression.

Even Sam finally concluded that the chandelier had to go. We would just have to find some way to scrape up the money for a replacement or else patch the ceiling, but that forest of glassy pretension and cankered brass was simply not going to hang over another Sunday dinner. The kids, however, raised a veritable howl of protest. Didn't we know that that was where Lawrence now slept at night?

Even if I had not heard that—and Sam was certainly not in any frame of mind to be told it—Granddaddy was determined. He would buy us a new light fixture as a gift, and Lawrence could take the hindmost. The children's protests degenerated into tears and then into genuine anxiety. Finally both men compromised. The old chandelier would be taken down, but it would be put up in the attic instead of out on the trash bins. Realizing that it was the best they were going to get, the girls settled, and our second fall progressed into our second winter. Lawrence continued to enter into their conversations from time to time, but life took up a routine and a pattern in which Lawrence, being merely a part, was less particular and less noticeable.

Over the years we were joined by John, then Wade, then Sam Jr., and finally Rebecca. We had long since restored the old house in midtown and modernized it, but even that was never going to make it large enough to hold us all comfortably. Granddaddy had died, and Grandma had come to live with us. It was just all too much. Moreover, Sam yearned for the country. His practice was established. There were partners to share the night call. I had, years before, given up teaching for writing, a profession better practiced in isolation than in community. The country was ideal from my point of view. The decision was made. We would leave the city and move as soon as we could.

Rebecca was two and immune to all the fuss of looking for a farm to buy, of finding a realtor who would fool with our multiplicities and clutter, and—most dreadful of all—of looking for a buyer, but the rest of us were in agony. With the restoration of the house and of the neighborhood, property values had shot way up; so had our rather sizeable cash investment in materials, repairs, and two additions. Consequently, not a lot of folks were both able to afford the house and young enough to want to take on what was always going to be "an older home."

Meanwhile we had found the farm, which was absolutely perfect. The kids loved it; Sam was radiant; and I was filled with a peace I have continued to feel ever since that first day when we walked onto the place and I knew I was home at last. It was right for us. If we could only sell that house! What we had once loved and been happy in became an albatross, a burden we couldn't unload.

It seemed to us that hundreds of people came through, looked, and left. Bet Brown, our realtor, was in despair after three months. She complained bitterly to me one afternoon that if she had to climb those attic stairs one more time, she thought she'd kill the client right there on the landing and wash her hands of the whole deal!

So it went, until the late spring day when the doorbell rang and I opened it to a middle-aged man. I looked at him, and a voice in my head said, "This is it!" And sure enough, it was. His realtor followed docilely behind him, but there was never any question that this was our buyer. We were tearful, we were so relieved. To the country we were going!

Three days later Bet brought the papers for us to sign. The older children watched fascinated as their father and I signed the copies that would relieve us of the house and make the farm possible. We stayed up late afterward and celebrated. What a happy festival we made there in the old kitchen's dim light! Then to bed and to a deep, heavy sleep. After so much anxiety for so long, it was the sweetest rest I could ever remember— until about four o'clock.

Suddenly there was the most alarming noise in the bathroom, followed by Mary's hollering, followed by a huge crash downstairs in the kitchen, followed by the attic door's flying open. Even Sam woke up for this one. Mary was standing in the middle of the hall, eighteen and as indignant as she could be. "Lawrence just pulled my toes!" She was livid, so livid her father didn't bother to argue with her.

The hall floor was covered with dirty clothes that had obviously been dragged out of the built-in clothes hamper in the front bathroom. Picking them up, I headed to the bathroom to put them back into the hamper. What hamper? The thing had been ripped literally out of the wall, the wooden door splintered and left wounded and useless in the floor of the bathroom. Sam glowered, but to his eternal credit let it be said that he never challenged the actuality of what we were looking at.

The attic door was plainly open, and Sam rebolted it as he turned back down the hall and headed for the kitchen, followed by the six Tickles who were big enough to have been awakened by the ruckus. The kitchen was a mess. The notes and bills and lists that had been magnetized to the refrigerator were strewn all over the floor. The freezer door was open, and the food had been spilled.

"Lawrence is mad. He just doesn't want us to leave." Mary was too big to paddle; I think that was the only thing that saved her, for Sam turned on her in a whirl. "Don't you ever say that again!"

She looked him straight in the eye. "But it's true." And she went about cleaning up.

Back upstairs I said to him, "Why?" and with much less sureness than he had shown downstairs, he answered me. "I don't know."

We moved uneventfully, uneventful as most moves go, that is. On the next to the last load, Laura said to her father that he had better go to the attic and get the chandelier. He was aghast. Why would we take that old thing? "You'd just better," she said. "It's where Lawrence still sleeps."

Sam absolutely refused until John, age seven, announced he wouldn't move unless the chandelier went. Defeated and/or politic in his choice of what ground to defend, Sam mounted the attic steps one last time to retrieve the chandelier. It was gone. The children didn't believe him, and there was a mass exodus up the rickety stairs to confirm the fact that he had not pulled a fast one. It was indeed gone. Even I went up just to be sure. John was cross, and Sam Jr. cried because Lawrence would have no place to sleep on the farm. Both accused Sam Sr. of having thrown the thing away. Even gentle Laura was suspicious of her father until his protestations convinced us that he simply hadn't even remembered the chandelier, much less thought enough about it to bother with disposing of it.

That afternoon Bet came by with the last of the warranties and the keys for the farmhouse. John immediately interrupted her errand with the tale of our lost chandelier. "No, honey," she reassured him, "it's up there behind the eaves and beyond the landing. I saw it week before last when I was up there for the last time."

He stoutly defended himself, and I assured her that the thing was really gone.

"Nonsense. Come on. I'll show you!" And Bet, who hated those stairs with fervor, was on her way.

In a few minutes she was back. "It's gone!" Her voice had a kind of hollow sound to it.

"I told you," said John.

"But it really was there when I made my last check of everything before we closed!"

"I know," I said. I had given up.

So, happy, but a bit less cheerful than we might otherwise have been, we moved without Lawrence and his chandelier, the last load being only us, the children, and the dog. We moved in June, put in a partial crop and started a herd that summer, and settled contentedly into remembered patterns of earlier years and earlier ways. Life was good. Mary went off to college for her first year. Nora and her husband had a baby boy, which did wonders for all of us. And I got up grateful every morning—consciously grateful—for where I was and who I was. No one thought of our situation as being life without Lawrence. He was never mentioned anymore.

Then one sunny morning in October the phone rang, and it was Bet Brown. "I have your ghost."

"What?"

"We have Lawrence, or I think we must. Someone keeps turning on the lights in the middle of the night. And this past week the TV in the den has been coming on about four o'clock every morning, blaring away until someone goes down and turns it off. Then last night it started with the radios. My husband says I have to do something."

"Do you have an attic?"

"Yeah, but the chandelier's not up there. My son already looked. It's like Lawrence is mad at me for selling the house."

I tried to be jovial. "I'm glad it's you and not me with this problem."

"Honestly," she snorted back at me. "I don't even believe in ghosts. But he really is doing this stuff . . . I mean, that really is why it's happening, isn't it?"

"I suspect so." I was struggling to be as detached as possible.

"Well, honestly!" And she hung up.

Two weeks later she called again. "Haven't you got any idea about what to do with this thing?"

"None."

"It's wearing us out! No one can sleep."

"I really am sorry, Bet." I could tell from the silence that she didn't believe me. "The only time we ever had trouble was the night we signed the papers and he went berserk. I honestly think it will get better all by itself." Then I added, "And I really do wish he'd come home," and realized I meant it.

"I just wish he'd *go* home!" Bet said and hung up emphatically.

Six weeks later, just at Christmas when the weather was still crisp but not yet bitter, Laura came sweetly into the kitchen for supper. "Guess who's in the side yard outside my window?"

No one should be! We were miles out in the country! "Who?" I asked in alarm.

"Lawrence!" She was plainly overjoyed.

"Are you sure?"

"Of course I'm sure!" And she was, because he was.

Within ten days John had seen him in the den, and I, looking down the steps one afternoon, had seen him in the lower hall. He turned and looked directly at me for the first time in all those years, and we made a kind of silent pact. He was home to stay. He may not like the country too well, but he liked us well enough to hang in there.

And so it has been in all the years since then. He comes and goes. The children and now the grandchildren speak of him as familiarly as they speak of one another.

Sam is still skittish of too much talk. More now than in our city years. I think he fears that we may all misunderstand what is happening, that in too ready a familiarity with whatever Lawrence is we may accept cheap or romantic explanations for him.

We are no longer young, nor are the children of our youth any longer young. We know more now, all of us, and we know enough to understand Sam's hesitancy about the easy explanations.

So I am not recording all these events casually or without reason. I am recording them because they are part of us certainly, part of the myth that is this one particular family. And partly because, being the only rift in time I have ever known personally, Lawrence has given me a lot more than Sam's doubt or the children's delight. He has taught me about myself.

You see, there are times when I don't even believe in Lawrence, and that scares me because I can remember other times, like that first time on the back stairs, when I believed in him most earnestly.

There are other times when I believe in Lawrence as an invention that has given the children and me, if not their father, great amusement and that has bonded us in a way that only myths can. I can remember all the Christmases, for instance, when someone would put a gift under the tree and sign the card, "From Lawrence," and we all knew it was a hoax even if we couldn't determine the hoaxer. But I also know that the fractured clothes hamper and Bet Brown's part of our story are absolutely true, and she will be the first to swear to it, believe me.

There are other times when I believe that Lawrence could well be just a projection of our emotional need for him. We were burglarized here once. An odd crime for the country. We considered it more of a possibility in the city, but it happened here. (And, indeed, almost

happened again within a month of our first experience.)
It would be hard to explain to anyone who has never
known that crime exactly how pervasive are its conse-
quences, especially for young children whose rooms
have been destroyed and whose toys have been
removed. There is no doubt that, when Bet Brown's
second call came, five weeks after our burglary and
three weeks after our burglar's second attempt at us, the
intensity of my response, of my wishing deeply that
Lawrence would come home to us, was born of an even
more intense and instantaneous realization that there
would be no more burglaries if he were to do so. And
that, too, is hard to confess publicly.

During the days of Ordinary Time there falls the
Feast of the Transfiguration. It is the church's remem-
brance of an otherworldly event in the life of our Lord
that was witnessed by three of his disciples:

> Jesus taketh with him Peter, and James, and
> John, and leadeth them up into an high mountain
> apart by themselves: and he was transfigured
> before them. And his raiment became shining,
> exceeding white as snow; so as no fuller on earth
> can white them. And there appeared unto them

Elias with Moses: and they were talking with Jesus.
(Mark 9:2–4)

As otherworldly as Lawrence has been for me, I have come to understand what he has given me. He has given me the liberating proof that I am out of my depth, that I am inconsistent, that I don't know how to use things that I both see and sometimes don't see. That understanding may be his greatest gift to us—the license to live in thankfulness with circumstances we cannot always either fathom or approve, for such is a building stone for miracles, that somehow it is all right to live not knowing how, but just using each day's particular version of things as being that day's particular truth.

CHAPTER 6

Of Creatures Kept and the Women Who Keep Them

I am not a fancier of flowers, at least not in the usual sense of that phrase. But I do have a rather considerable fondness for geraniums, probably due more to their acrid odor and vibrant color than to the fact that they are flowers.

Women learn early that anything that is alive is a potential and probable responsibility. As a result we become very selective about which flora and fauna to accept, and we become very analytical about our own selection processes. Thus my relative sureness that the odor of a thing matters to me; for the smell of geraniums,

I would water and prune anything every day for the rest of my life.

Geraniums happily have yet another virtue that endears them to me: they attract everything, and every summer their pots become a display of life on a miniature scale. The first year we came to the farm to live, I confess I bought geraniums at the feed store to try to give some liveliness to our front porch. That structure, which faces southeast into the early morning heat, suffers from the impoverishment of size and grace that often characterizes southern houses and that leads to the wondrous piece of vocabulary, the *stoop*. I never have quite known whether the house was supposed to stoop to meet the inelegance of its entryway or whether the whole was so compromised by the roofless blob of poured concrete as to make its owner want to stoop. Whichever the way of the thing, we have a stoop just big enough to accommodate two small stands and two pots of geraniums.

Warmed by the morning sun and kept breathlessly toasty by the brick and concrete around them, the geraniums of our first year flourished with uncontrollable abandon, and I became quite attached to their courage and good humor. The children likewise shared my sense of pleasure in the heartiness of the flowers. With the coming of fall we were so bonded to the pots of color as to be unwilling to give them over to their demise. Sam set one pot in the garage window to take the winter sun in a more secluded and sheltered environment. The other he set on a contrived ledge in the kitchen window to appease the children and me.

The window, like most kitchen ones, sits in the dead center of a double sink, and ours looks out over the backyard and the lower pastures toward the pond. Doing dishes isn't my favorite chore, but the view from the window is one of my choice pleasures. As a result I have always managed to dawdle over the dishes in the best of times. The addition of the geranium pot that first October further slowed the washing-up process.

For the first week or two, the geranium was as lush inside as it had been out on the stoop. By the first of November, though, it was beginning to show withdrawal symptoms, and its leaves were less thick, its blooms less vivid. Sam fertilized both pots and waited.

A week later—the weather already chilly and the view turning gray into the winter vista—I was washing the pots and loading the dishwasher when I had an overwhelming sense of someone or something staring at me. The sensation was not eerie or unpleasant, just persistent. I shook it off and closed down the kitchen for the evening.

The next morning I was drawing water for the teakettle when the same sense of presence overcame me. I shortened my sights this time (it was the cold light of day now) and looked at the geranium. Sitting placidly on the edge of the pot was a baby frog. Only his throat was moving, but he was studying me with all the sobriety and intensity of a Martian on his first trip to earth. The obvious superiority of his stance was disconcerting, but his presence was charming. I made a move toward him, and he was as quickly gone back into the pot. I called Sam and the children to come and see, but nowhere could we detect any evidence of a frog. In fact, Sam teased me by explaining to the children that I was, as they all knew, a perpetual dreamer and romantic. In part, I think, he believed his own story.

The day ended as all days do, and once more I closed down the kitchen without incident. The frog was forgotten by everyone except me. I went up to read in bed, leaving Sam to work as he did each night on the kitchen table with his medical records and reading. About midnight he came upstairs laughing and insisting that I wake up. Above his poking and chuckling, I could distinctly hear downstairs the croaking of a frog. "Nearly scared me to death the first time!" was Sam's comment as I got up to go and see. And there on the rim of the pot sat our visitor, for all the world looking as if he owned the place.

The next morning the frog came up to the rim from under the leaves as soon as I turned on the kitchen lights. By breakfast the children had agreed to name him Jeremiah since that was during the years when a popular song featured a bullfrog named Jeremiah. And Jeremiah was admitted to our lives as a permanent resident.

The children and I could not for the life of us figure out what Jeremiah was eating, but he definitely was growing to rather impressive proportions. By December he had become a full-size frog with a deep throttling kind of croak. He was silent as a church mouse as long as someone was in the kitchen with him. The minute, however, that everyone left the kitchen, Jeremiah raised his protest with all the ferocity of a nine-month-old baby put down for a nap. Even the lights did not fool him. He wanted human companionship at all times, period. Eventually we simply learned to sleep in spite of the croaking; and Jeremiah, like a bright child, got smart enough to give up his nighttime protest, restricting his demands to those for daytime company. That was easier for us to accommodate, and we fell into a comfortable arrangement of living together.

As he grew older, Jeremiah gained a certain fastidiousness that the children found humorous and that I found somewhat less appealing. Every morning when I came into the kitchen to begin breakfast, Jeremiah arose from his geranium bed, hopped to the rim of the pot, turned around with his face to the center of the pot, and defecated onto the kitchen windowsill. That chore accomplished for the day, he turned around to watch me studiously as I cleaned up the mess he had just made. It was an interesting way to begin the day.

As a present and in an attempt to encourage such exquisite concern for cleanliness, Sam gave Jeremiah a bathtub of his own for Christmas. The children were mystified as Sam emptied one of those sample pill bottles that doctors get by the hundreds, cut it into halves lengthwise, sealed the semicircular neck with bathtub caulk, and then set it in Jeremiah's pot. The minute Sam filled the contrivance with water, it was clear that Jeremiah at least was not mystified by the gift; and thereafter he added an extended bath to his morning routine.

It was, in fact, the bathtub that also solved the mystery of Jeremiah's increasing corpulence. One morning Jeremiah seemed hesitant to jump into his swimming pool. He sat looking pointedly at it, but he would not get in. Curious, I lifted a geranium leaf to investigate and found only a bit of trash in the water. I lifted it out and discovered to my surprise that it was a bit of raw hamburger which had inadvertently made its way into the tub. The question of Jeremiah's diet was resolved, and I was reasonably sure I could guess at his supplier.

Late that night as I lay reading in bed, I heard the refrigerator door open. Skipping downstairs quietly, I watched as Sam set at least a dozen tiny dots of raw meat carefully into the pot. "I thought so," I said from the kitchen doorway, and he at least had the grace to blush.

By mid-January Jeremiah was beginning to feel his oats. He took to jumping out of the pot for little side trips around the sink. We would find him looking at us from the watering pot or sitting on top of the kitchen matches. Then came the inevitable day when he discovered the joys of jumping, not to mention the joys of being good at it. He leaped from the sill to the stove, narrowly missing a pot of simmering beans.

Sam called a family conference. If we kept Jeremiah, we obviously stood a chance of losing him to an unattractive death by boiling or frying. If we let him out to the elements, we stood a chance of his death by inability to survive what he had never known in more clement times. The children voted to take their chances inside. By now the thought of losing him was as painful to them as to us. So, many a time during February and March someone had to grab a frog in midcareen. We became rather proficient at it actually, and I still think Jeremiah may be the reason John became so adept as a catcher. Early training can do a lot for a child.

But then April came. The light grew brighter and the days longer. The geranium began to bud and Jeremiah to decline. Hormones had obviously got him. He bellowed with a new and mournful call, like a foghorn with a chest cold. He refused to come out to the countertops and eventually to come to the rim. When for three days he refused even his good housekeeping practices, we knew it was time to face the facts of due process.

Sam and Rebecca took the geranium out and set it in the grass at the base of the front steps. For days Rebecca went faithfully every day to water the flower and the frog, and to talk to Jeremiah. For days he was there every time she went. Then there came the afternoon when he was not in the pot. She was dejected, but her despair evaporated when he reappeared in the pot by evening. And so it went for three or four weeks, Jeremiah gone during the days but home to sleep.

Just as I had decided that we might indeed keep him, there came the dusk when he did not return to his pot. For four or five days Rebecca watered and hoped, but Jeremiah was gone . . . until she found him living in the flowerbed surrounded by a veritable tribe of frogs. There was no question that it was Jeremiah, however, and she was content somehow to release him to his own. They spent the summer together, she and Jeremiah, having conversations across the porch railing about how things were in the flowerpot, but Jeremiah was no longer a part of our lives at any intimate level.

And in the years since then, the geraniums have continued to house a variety of creatures. One summer it was a ferociously beautiful war spider whose egg sac was the size of a small apple by the time winter came. Another year it was a kitten with a fondness for the warm pot and the pungent odor of the bruised stems. One summer we housed a swallow family. The mother, gliderlike and glossy dark in her swoops around the porch, completely filled the area under the leaves with her nest and closed the whole thing over at the top to the most narrow opening possible. I always checked to see whether or not she was home before I watered the plant, but sometimes it was impossible to detect her through the narrow opening. One day I miscalculated and watered while she was home, causing her enormous agitation. The next morning she was back in her pot, apparently having decided to forgive me my error.

During the dry, heavy days of that particular August, the gloss of swallow wings and waxy red brightness of the geraniums brightened the stoop and gave a lilt to my steps in the mornings. They reminded me that nurturing living things was womanliness for me. August 15 is the Feast of St. Mary the Virgin, and I observed it that year mindful of how all those creatures who had lived in the geranium pot had brought with them life that had stopped awhile and then passed on through my life. In this, we ladies—Mary and I—find our sisterhood as well as a holy commonality.

CHAPTER 7

The Cross and Other Icons

For centuries the celebration of the central symbol of our faith got caught up in the fuss over whether or not the real cross and its wood still existed and, if so, where. Most of us now are content to say that the answers to that dilemma are yes and everywhere. In the same way that the risen Lord exists in the bread and wine, so does his cross exist among us in all its holy uses. The eyes of conversion looking, see. Thus it has always been and will always be.

The Roman Catholic Church eventually placed Holy Cross Day on the fourteenth of September. In more recent times and for reasons I have never been privy to, other denominations like Lutheranism and

Episcopalianism that had never observed Holy Cross at all suddenly began to add the festival to their parish calendars.

Christian writers and theologians have often observed that we tend to see Christ as a hero, a great man in history, one comparable to Abe Lincoln or Gandhi—one worthy of inclusion in History 101, in other words. Of all the places one could file the Son of God, History 101 is probably the safest, the one most likely to demythologize him right down to Mahatma's battles or Ole Abe's level of honesty. The trouble seems to be, however, that while our intentions may be able to wedge Christ—literally as well as metaphorically—into a college syllabus on great human beings, even the bravest of us can't quite shove his cross in after him.

It doesn't fit very well, apparently because it stayed after he ascended. Call that cross whatever you will—amulet, icon, relic, symbol—it still hangs around our necks and on our walls, marks our mercy as well as our worship, sanctifies our holy places, and in corruptions of its form salutes the dark ones. Everywhere visible, it will do all things, in fact, except be domesticated by our culture.

It is fair to ask how an icon, a symbol, can make any notable difference in a person's ordinary life. I won't attempt to explain this theologically (I doubt that is really possible anyway). But I have my own story of icons that has made religion—and even the cross—a bit more understandable, at least to me.

It happened with my dressing table. It seems so simple now, but it was both frightening and very disconcerting at the time.

Rebecca had started school at last. For the first time in twenty-five years, I was at home alone for part of the day, free to play without interruption for five delicious hours among my pots and pans, my closets and linens, my books and files. Always before, when I would begin to straighten and organize, clean out, throw away, or decorate, Sam would say, "You're nesting again!" and I would realize abruptly and with joy that he was right— I was late—had been late for two or three weeks, sometimes a month.

With us, the ordering of life always announced the beginning of life as well. Or, to put it the other way around, new life always presented itself at our house by ordering the old one we already had. It was always somewhere between a joke and an irony for me that it was a medical household in which such a nonmedical system worked; but Sam always shrugged it off, his step lighter and his grin bigger each time he was right.

So the sorting of toys and the storing of clothes, the cataloging of books and the tossing of old dishes were always followed without comment or remark after that by the changing of the kindergartener to a bed, the toddler to a junior bed, the baby to a trundle, and the addition of a new bumper pad and a fresh mattress cover for the crib. Each new Tickle arrived to clean closets, scrubbed shelves, and organized drawers, none of which mattered a whit to him or her. But everyone else was terribly grateful since, for at least eighteen more months, it was most unlikely that I would feel the urge to sort us out again.

But this time it was different. Sam cocked his head when he saw the new scarf draped over the dresser, but he didn't say anything. Actually I didn't say anything either, because I didn't know what to say. In fact, I wanted to say something like "What's happening to me?" but that seemed like a silly, almost melodramatic way to start a conversation about a dresser scarf. It wasn't the scarf anyway; it was my compulsion to get it that I wanted to talk about and couldn't.

It was one of those sunny days of early fall when my obsession was born. Rebecca had been in kindergarten more than a month, and I had discovered the luxury of buying groceries alone—and in the daylight! From that discovery it had been a quick hop to discovering that I could buy cosmetics and bath supplies somewhere *besides* the grocery store, and also in the daylight. I was, in fact, buying hand lotion and cold cream when I thought suddenly to myself, *I can have them both out on a dresser now!*

It was an easy progression from there to realizing that I could move the bedroom lowboy to a place under the mirror near the bed and have a dresser again! A place of my own. Not a room, mind you, but a little place, a kind of shrine to my memory of how those adult women of my childhood had looked and smelled and honored themselves.

There in the store, I put down the hand lotion and abandoned the cold cream without even picking it up. I didn't want those functional bottles and ordinary brands. I didn't know what I did want, but I knew I would recognize it when I saw it . . . and I knew that I had to have the scarf first.

For almost three weeks after I had moved the lowboy into place under the mirror, I tried to find a scarf for it.

I went through every catalog we had on hand. (In the country, the catalog is still the store of choice, even for finery like dresser scarves.) When that didn't work, I went into the city one day and wandered through two department stores, but nothing drew me to it, mainly I think because I was so self-absorbed with trying to figure out why I was doing this, why everything else in my life was totally arrested until I could find a dresser scarf.

Then one day, just before the Thanksgiving holidays began, I found it. It was in my linen closet, folded away in the horde of leftovers I had packed away when Mrs. Tickle and later my own mother had broken up housekeeping. It was the simplest piece of hemmed cotton, very plain but very soft from myriad washings. In its plainness it was perfect, and I gave a little squeeze of thanks to whichever grandmother or aunt or cousin had made it.

Once back in the bedroom I was horrified to realize that my fingers were shaking, so great was my need to get the scarf in place before the school bus could bring me an audience. And it was just that! I didn't want the children to see me doing this thing, sanctifying this place. I didn't want to share it with them either, this sense of having made from memory and self a thing, an object, a concrete geography. Not yet. Later, when I was surer perhaps, but not now. So Sam only cocked his head, and I, escaping unchallenged, was left both anxious for, and afraid of, the children's questions.

Because I really was out of lotion and cleansing cream, I had to make the next move before the holidays could overtake me. More settled this time, more sure that whatever this was about was all right, I drove back to the city and walked among the cosmetic counters. Since I almost never used cosmetics and then badly, I didn't have to waste time testing them. I only had to look at them, knowing absolutely that the right color and shape would make themselves known.

Sure enough, there for more money than I had spent in my entire life for cosmetics sat a most substantial set of glazed jars with gold letters and handsome aquamarine lids of just the correct fulsomeness and excellence. Without batting an eye, I asked the consultant behind the counter, "Do you have hand lotion and cold cream in this line?" She did. The bottles were perfect in their square shapes with their rounded corners and their incised lettering.

Once back at home, my hands shook again. They should have been moved by the enormity of the price I had just paid out of a budget full of children to feed and educate. But the shaking was perfunctory, and I knew it. It was born more of excitement than guilt, and I knew that, too. Something very right was happening here, and whatever it was, it pleased me with its sense of serious health, not waste.

Because I got away with the scarf and the bottles, I became bolder. I swapped my everyday tissues for one of those square, flowered boutique boxes of colored ones. Nothing happened. No reaction from husband or children.

I took a Limoges candy dish—a wedding present I had packed away years before to keep it out of the way of little hands—from the storage closet and set it on the new dresser, filling it with lipsticks, hairpins, and combs, just as my mother and Sam's had done so many years before.

It was the afternoon after I had put the lipsticks in the dish that Rebecca finally said something. She came into our room where I was sewing and just looked. Then she said, very softly, "Could I please see your lipsticks?" She who, as recently as the day before yesterday, had been death to lipsticks was suddenly asking, and asking with a near reverence.

It was her reverence, of course, that told me what was happening. "Yes, you may."

She took a tube, opened it, looked at herself in the mirror, and then closed the lipstick, saying as she screwed it back down into its tube, "I guess I'll wait awhile." Then, "I'll just take some lotion instead." But she didn't. She just stood there a minute or two more considering herself in the mirror, and then, without saying anything else, she left.

Over the years I added a set of makeup brushes, which I have never used because I don't know how. I bought them because of the rich feel of the case they are in and because of the flower cart depicted so exquisitely on its top. I also added one of those elegant sets of Chinese stacking boxes to hold my favorite necklaces. I chose the set not for its usefulness, however, but because its serene designs and brilliant lacquered red make me happy with life and with Asian luck.

There are times now—many times, in fact—when I just sit in the sewing chair and rock, looking at the dresser with its icons of perfumes and creams, its vessels of pins and baubles, its simple cloth and lacquered reliquary. I rock and look and am always more and more at one with the new lift that began with the ordering of the dresser, more grateful for the slipping into things that this altar gave me.

As I go forward into what my mother was when I first remember her, and as I watch her granddaughters and great-granddaughters work to become us both, I disappear into creams and odors and pins just as, from the beginning of the whole thing, I think I must have known that I would. When by the grace of God the things that became the symbols become things once more, neither they nor we are the same, nor have we changed. It is the use of even the simplest sort of icon to teach us that, I suspect.

CHAPTER 8

How Beautiful upon the Mountains

Ember Days in the church year are dedicated to prayers for the clergy—to thanksgiving for them, to petitions for their increase, and to requests for their spiritual sustenance. Although historically the Ember Days were observed four times throughout the year, over the decades of the last century they have been most actively observed in the autumn.

As an omission or a diminishment of the liturgical calendar, the loss of the Ember Days never really troubled me much because they didn't signify anything that had been privately and emotionally important to me. But one year our church was without a pastor for ten months, and my appreciation and concern for our clergy deepened significantly during that period.

Most of us had never been without a pastor before. Midway through the months that we were unpastored, I took an informal poll after services one Sunday. I had to know if I were the only one in the place who found ours to be a distressing situation. I was relieved to discover that I was not alone—most of us had no idea of how to run a parish without a priest and absolutely no prior experience to draw on for help, especially not in a fairly small and fairly rural parish.

The usual and obvious things happened on schedule, of course. I mean that the lights were on, so apparently the junior warden was paying the bills. Bill Bains's elaborate spice garden and flowering borders continued to thrive in the churchyard. (They were oblivious to the need for any blessing except the ones that fell on them constantly from Bill's hands, I suppose.) There was always at least one service each Sunday, so either the senior warden or the bishop must not have forgotten that we existed.

I never did figure out who was doing our burying and our marrying because, selfishly but fortunately, neither we nor anyone I knew had occasion for either function. (Country parishes are rather healthy in the long run and not much given to hasty marriages. If my memory serves me correctly, however, the new priest performed three weddings in the first month after his arrival, but that is beside the point.) Baptisms we did on Sundays with the interim preacher of the day serving as officiant. Since baptisms are so poignant in and of themselves, I have always held that who the officiant is matters almost not at all.

But despite all the apparent routine and the surface tranquility, things began to change for us in those ten months. The size of the congregation dwindled more each Sunday, as did the size of the choir until it got down to a soloist for a Sunday or two toward the end of things. Since no one I know really goes to church to see the preacher, I found this diminution hard to explain. Yet I, too, felt its pull, its call to lie dormant because the parish felt dormant.

Holy days were not kept. For the first time in my adult life, day after day peeled off my kitchen calendar uncelebrated and unmarked save by private prayer at home. On Wednesday nights, the only church lights were the arc lights in the parking lot. Daily offices went unsaid. As a community, we fainted and were scattered abroad as sheep having no shepherd, a piece of Scripture I never had appreciated until I watched it happening around me.

Then he came. Our new rector. "How beautiful upon the mountains the feet of them that bring glad tidings"—

another piece of Scripture that I never had really appreciated until I got to watch it happening around me.

It was gradual, you understand. No major events, no dancing in the parish hall. It was all very quiet and very subtle. The first thing I noticed actually was almost inconsequential. Grown men, all of them perfectly capable of having acted on their own without direction, suddenly decided one Saturday to spend the afternoon trimming the edges of the parking lot and poisoning the grass that over the past few months had broken its way into the asphalt in at least two dozen places. *Interesting*, I thought, *that none of us had seen it all summer or worried about it.*

The next thing I knew, there were people I had never seen before coming to Sunday services. Where he found them I may never know. And though I came to know many of them eventually, I couldn't imagine just outright asking someone, "Where were you when he found you?" much as I would have liked to.

Then the back row, and shortly after that the two back rows, began to fill up with babies, or with families with babies. If you sat anywhere in the back third of the nave, you were destined not to hear any single sermon in its entirety. You did gain, however, an overwhelming sense of our future as a body of God's faithful.

The next thing was that the holy days came back, not only the big ones we were accustomed to having but also the little ones that we weren't, the so-called lesser feasts and fasts. Six weeks into the new cleric, one of my friends in the altar guild sighed to me as we were leaving services one evening. "My goodness, he's going to church us to death!" I looked at her, and we both laughed out loud like those who have discovered water in the middle of a drought.

Or maybe I should say food in the middle of a famine. I had truly not realized how derelict we had become about the transient poor and homeless until the parish kitchen began once more to fill up with donations of canned goods. And I had forgotten how much I despised those tacky containers that sit on our supper table and say "Pennies for Hunger" until Rebecca triumphantly set one there and said, "See what we've got again!" It was fed more by her change and allowance than by anyone else among us, so great was her pleasure in once more having a priest to collect and use it. So the changes occurred, and we rejoiced.

I had occasion to drive to the cathedral one day and was greeted by the bishop as I went in the narthex door. In passing, he asked me how I liked our new rector, and I heard myself responding, "Just great, but it's a little like watching the Roto-Rooter man at work." He looked a bit nonplussed and I certainly felt it, but I knew I had said, albeit unthinkingly, exactly what I meant. Debris and obstacles and inertia just weren't there anymore.

My metaphor came back to me one day when I went to Morning Prayer and saw the hole in the back wall of our parish house. It certainly looked like a Roto-Rooter had hit it. In truth, it turned out that the vestry had approved the funds to expand the parish hall now instead of later; it appeared that we had outgrown the present one rather dramatically, and way ahead of previous projections.

Yes, Lord, I thought to myself, *we do indeed have a new priest at our house.* And that Ember Day it wasn't hard at all for me to pray for more of the same. How beautiful upon everything everywhere are the feet of them that bring good tidings; that publish peace; that say unto us, "Thy God reigneth!" Especially of Roto-Rooter men.

CHAPTER 9

Of Bulls and Angels

Always referred to at our house by its shortened name of Michaelmas, the Feast of St. Michael and All Angels is still my favorite holy day, even in my adulthood.

There is something glorious about the fall in and of itself. It demands almost nothing of us except our applause. Save for putting up the hay and gathering in the last of the vegetables for preserving, the hard chores are done until the first freeze comes. The world is still warm, but comfortably so for the first time in months; and the chilly evenings speak only of the exhilaration of winter, not of its risks and dangers. So there is in Michaelmas the kind of natural stimulation of the senses that has always pleased me anyway.

But then suddenly, right in the safety of those warm days, cool nights, and lightened workloads comes the most perplexing and titillating set of questions in orthodox Christianity. What is the nature of the angels? What is their use and place in the scheme of things? What is their relationship to us? What is their ordinary and customary dwelling? Christ certainly refers to them again and again as active agents in his world. Christian after earnest Christian within my own acquaintance as well as outside it has certainly tried to deny them any function in his or her world. In fact, the majority of Christendom celebrates only St. Michael on this day; the Anglican Church adds "all angels." So what of angels?

Uncomfortable with them and yet convinced of their scriptural basis, most of us approach each Michaelmas hoping more for enlightenment than for anything else, I suspect . . . and reveling in the sweet excitement of knowing we won't receive it, at least not directly, immediately, or tangibly.

But one autumn, my children and I witnessed the world beyond this one in the context of ordinary life among our farm creatures. That day the realm of angels and all things unknowable opened up for me just a little bit more.

The late September sunshine, benign and dry, glowed quietly over the years and the meadows beyond as we drove into the drive and parked. Like the children. I was looking forward to this week of interrupted routine, of holiday from all the schedules and chores that I should follow but don't whenever escape is possible.

We had just put Sam on an airplane for a week of meetings in Boston. For me that meant supper would be sandwiches, not an entree and vegetables—fifteen minutes not ninety, in other words. Time to read. Tomorrow night, frozen dinners. Monday night? We would see how we all felt by then.

For the two boys it meant a definite laxity about the grass. Wait until Friday to cut it again; it doesn't grow all that fast in September. A certain casualness about the hens' nests; they can run a week without new pine needles. A tendency to let the last of the okra get too large to be worth picking, the peppers too red, the eggplants too wormy. A lot of fishing down at the pond, however. Now there was a crop that needed to be garnered while there was still time!

For Rebecca, the youngest at age nine, the prospect was less heady. She alone faced the next six days with hesitation. Our chores and routines were not yet her burdens; rather they were the definitions of her days. Daddy's big hands and hearty hugs, like his long talks with her while they planted and pruned and harvested, were the mirrors in which she saw herself as engaging, accomplished, precious beyond all other things in life. And I, remembering from past experience, knew that after the sandwiches had been eaten and the book enjoyed for an hour or two, those intimate hours of the night would come, and I, too, would be as morose as she and for much the same reasons.

So we parked the car, and ideal day or not, we went into the house—I to wash up the breakfast mess we had left to get to the airport on time, the boys to fall dead in sleeping bags in front of the Saturday morning TV. Only Rebecca veered off to the field. *Like Electra mourning*, I thought to myself as I watched her through the kitchen window. She wandered aimlessly along the fence line, crawled through finally, and started toward the pond. I finished the dishes and was thinking sinfully of skipping the laundry in favor of a manuscript I was working on, when I saw Rebecca come back over the hillock from the pond. "Something's wrong with Saint's calf," she said as she came in the back door. "It's just standing at the pond bawling."

"Oh, I wouldn't worry about it," I answered. "She's just looking for her mama to feed her."

"I don't think so," she said, with the kind of calm that I have long since learned to believe instantly when it occurs in children. I looked at her and then looked out toward the pasture. As I watched, I saw cow after cow move laboriously over the crest of the hillock and come to stand at the fence, looking toward the house. That also is a gesture that years of living with animals has made me respect in them. There was something wrong, or they would not have come for us.

I called for the boys, both of whom protested viciously that this was supposed to be their free Saturday. "Give us a break, Ma" was the chorus, but there was to be no break.

The cows parted as the four of us climbed back through the fence, following the bawling of the calf as it led us toward the pond. Halfway down the sloping pasture stood the calf. Two weeks old and a beauty. Much too old and pretty, I suddenly realized, to look wobbly and weak. Something was wrong. What Rebecca had sensed intuitively I could give adult reason to: that calf had not been fed in at least twelve hours. Beside me I heard fourteen-year-old

John mutter, "Oh, boy," and I knew that he had reached the same conclusion.

Behind us the herd had reassembled, waiting for something. The calf began to move, and Rebecca started after her. "Wait!" I grabbed her arm. "Let the calf go." We watched her as she wobbled off toward the east meadow below the barn. Slowly the herd began to break and follow. We did likewise. And there, on the rise just beyond the cow path to the feeding racks, lay Saint on her side, legs stuck stiffly out in front of her, eyes open, flies already eating around her face. As we watched, the calf walked over and tried once more to nurse the stiffened udder. The herd moved off, as if totally disinterested now that we had been led to the spot. *Like gossips, they just love a tragedy!* I thought bitterly as I began to figure dully what all this meant to our intended holiday.

The first necessity obviously was to get some milk into the calf. I sent John back to get some rope, and Sam Jr. and Rebecca to open up the smallest stall in the barn and get some hay spread out. It had been three or four years since I had tried to manhandle a calf. I had forgotten how hard they can kick and how tough a ride it can be to hold one. This one might be weak and young, but she had no intention of being caught, much less hauled away from her mother. We finally got her down, her legs lashed somewhat inexpertly, and the whole thrashing mass back to the barn. For two hours we struggled, as one always must, with a calf who did not—most definitely did not—like the feel of the rubber nipple or the taste of the milk replacement we were forcing on her. Finally she ate enough to allow us to go back in for the sandwiches that did not seem nearly so attractive after all.

As lunch ended, John asked the question we had been trying to avoid all morning. What about Saint? Saturday and no one to call for extra help. Leaving her where she was would bring the coyotes and wild dogs up from the Loosahatchie Bottoms and into the pasture. Once there, they would kill the calves as soon as they had finished the carcass. Burying her would be impossible without the backhoe that none of us could operate. I thought of Boston and meetings and wondered how we could have been so foolish as to look forward to this week without structure. Well, obviously we had to move her. I remembered that once, Sam had disposed of a yearling by taking the body down to a natural depression at the foot of the meadow where the close began, setting it in the little eroded valley just at the edge of the uncleared bog. We still wouldn't be strong enough to dig sufficient earth to bury her, but we could at least get her half-buried and away from the vulnerable younger cattle, assuming we could contrive a way to move her there.

Back to the field we went, John driving the pickup ahead of the rest of us. He negotiated the terracing and hills with a skill far beyond that of most boys his age, and I felt not only the swell of pride that comes to women who have produced good male children, but also the sense of wonder that recognizes—abruptly and humbly—that those skills were not self-taught. They were learned, acquired, taught by the man who, though absent in Boston, was still working the pasture with us at that very moment. *The eternal line of maleness, unbroken and unbreakable*, I thought, as I watched him back the truck up and begin to maneuver it into alignment, back bumper even with the outstretched legs of the carcass.

Suddenly over the rise I saw the bull move heavily and forcefully up the slope and toward the truck. Long since turned into a useful pet—loved on, stroked, and scratched upon every occasion—the bull was certainly nothing to be concerned about. John continued to move the truck as the bull moved deliberately toward us. A little uneasy somehow, I picked up Rebecca and told Sam Jr. to jump into the bed of the truck. Still the bull came toward us. I called to John to pull away— "Give him room!" And John pulled the truck down twenty feet or so from the cow, parked it, and crawled into the truck bed with his brother. I slid Rebecca back down to the ground beside me. Whatever this was all about, there was no danger to us if we were still.

Solemnly over the hill came the rest of the herd. I backed off farther, holding Rebecca's hand as we watched. The herd stopped at the top of the ridge, watching the scene below them. The bull approached Saint, running his nose along her now distended underside. He snorted the flies off her head, walked around her full circle once, and then began ritually to mount the carcass. She was too long dead, of course, to admit of penetration, and the effort was not that which usually accompanies mating. It was, ultimately, ritualistic.

Farm children learn early the purposes of sex; they also learn early to reverence the emotions of it. All three of ours watched with quietness—not a word said in the whole meadow—while the bull dismounted and stood to one side. As we watched, he raised his head and looked across the fields with a magnificence that becomes a king. Coal black and polished by the fall sun, he uttered a sound I had never before heard from a bull, a kind of call to the herd that was summons, explanation, and completion. Then, as simply as he had begun, he lowered his head and moved on toward the close.

For whatever reason—and I shall never know what it was or what set of peculiar circumstances had contrived to permit it—we had been witness to something that, I have since learned, few farmers are ever allowed to see. Like Jacob on the fields of Luz, we had watched the customs and conventions of a life as complete as our own—one with which for years we had shared daily space and purpose, but one which we had, until that afternoon, never seen. Like Jacob, too, we knew we were on holy ground. We had been in Bethel; we had been witness to the mysteries of another order. Through the tears in my eyes, I looked down and saw Rebecca swipe at hers with her forearm.

The herd slowly came down the rise toward us. Most of them paused to smell the carcass with their lowered noses; they all moved toward the bull, who still waited for them in the shade of the close. Once there, they followed the way of cows and settled down to doze in the fading sun as if nothing had happened. The bull alone stood watching us.

Without asking, John swung back into the cab and cranked the motor. Adroitly he put the truck back into position and lifted out the lengths of rope he had brought from the barn. Together, with Rebecca and Sam Jr. watching, we lashed the stiffened legs together and then to the hitch on the back of the truck and began the tedious process of, inch by inch, dragging the body down to the edge of the bog. With nothing said, Sam Jr. picked up a pole, and the three of us, once the body was unlashed, rolled the last of Saint down into the gully below.

Rebecca and I walked back to the house while the boys finished and parked the truck. Without thinking, I began to chop salad and season a quart of beans. There would be leftover fried chicken, and I could throw some biscuits in the oven. *An entree and vegetables*, I thought to myself. Sam Jr. came in and silently picked up the garden basket. I saw him a few minutes later picking the okra in the garden. Far to the front I heard John turn over the motor on the lawn tractor. We would have a trim yard for Sunday after all. Supper would be ready in a little while, then baths and to rest. Tomorrow would be Michaelmas—the Feast of St. Michael and All

Angels—the one day of the year when all Christendom pays at least lip service to invisible realities and unseen orders. We who had been so subtly instructed would likewise be ordered and ready when the words of the Book of Common Prayer began tomorrow morning's worship: "O Everlasting God, who hast ordained and constituted the ministries of angels and men in a wonderful order . . ."

CHAPTER 10

Haying

S till not admitted to the status of red-letter saint outside the Roman Catholic Church, St. Francis of
Assisi is, nonetheless and hands down, still the best-
known and most loved of Christian saints, even among
non-Christians.

Born in A.D. 1181 or 1182 to the Bernardone family of
Assisi in Italy, John (his baptismal name) early developed
such a passion for the troubadour songs and elaborate
ways of French culture that he soon came to be known as
Il Francesco, "the Little Frenchman," a name that was to
stick with him for the rest of Western time.

Though in conversion and rapture the Little
Frenchman lost his absorption with Gallic luxury, he
never lost his sense of wonder in the natural world or
his exquisite union with all his Father's creatures and

creations. In a rural parish like ours, as in many a city one as well, St. Francis stands in blessing near the narthex door.

And in our parish, as in a growing number of parishes across America, the children come, bringing with them their pets, for the services that always conclude with, and are occasioned by, the Blessing of the Animals. Only King David himself ever had as keen an understanding of the interface between the Creator and the Creator's world as St. Francis, unless it is the children whose pets the priest blesses on this autumn day. Yet it is a union that I can remember feeling and that country living sometimes grants me again on brief occasions.

I remember one particular autumn weekend. We were haying. It was a task that changed almost not at all from one autumn to the next, or from one generation to another. Seven hundred and fifty bales that were scattered over the ground on Friday would, by nightfall Sunday, be tightly wedged and stacked into the loft, the empty paddocks, and the side corridors of the barn.

Philip, still single but living now in the city, had come home for the weekend to help drive the trucks. A neighbor from around the bend had brought his truck and his son. They would also spend the whole weekend here, working alongside the two hired hands, my husband, and the younger boys.

The only real difference between our weekend and the haying days of a hundred years before was that our hay was bought and hauled in rather than grown on the place. Land had become too costly now for most of us to be able to use it for growing feed. Frequently the hay was bought from the acreage along the interstates or from the grasslands under antennas and electric lines or from the fallow pastures of absentee landlords. Ours that year was coming from around a radio installation on the edge of the city.

Day labor, as always, was contracted on the side from among the men who followed the balers in the hope of picking up a day or two of extra work over the weekend. Most of them were men who grew up in the country and moved to town to work in jobs at factories or on assembly lines. They followed the balers as much for the chance to engage in remembered physical tasks and to acquire fresh produce from the farmer's garden as for the extra money they would earn. Sometime that weekend I would manage to get out to the garden and harvest enough bell peppers, hot peppers, eggplant, and okra to satisfy them and their families for the three days' work. It would be the one pleasant task of my weekend, for like my grandmother and my great-grand-mothers before me, I would spend the three days— except for the stolen moments in the garden and the few hours of sleep—in the kitchen.

Again that year I would have unremitting company there as well. Rebecca was ten, still too young and too petite to go out in the fields while the trucks and the men were moving the bales, so she was confined all weekend to the house and to the parameters of my eyes and ears. Like me, she would grow cross and restless as the hours wore on. Eventually, we both knew, there would come the last run late on Sunday afternoon when Sam would come for her, and she would ride the trucks in for the last load. Later she would sit triumphantly on the hood of the truck while the men forced the last few bales into the bloated paddocks. Until that magic hour of privilege came, she was stuck indoors with me, and she knew it. We both would pay the price of her sense of being excluded.

By ten o'clock on Saturday I was already making the fourth pitcher of iced tea and uncapping the fifth dou-ble liter of Coca-Cola. The thermoses had just come in the back door covered—like fifteen-year-old John, who

had brought them—in straw and mud and sweat. I
cleaned them again, replenished the ice, poured the tea
and the Coke, sent out more plastic cups and retrieved
the last load for washing. He waited laconically by the
back door, enjoying his brief rest and the shade, hoping
I wouldn't hurry. By midafternoon I would be adding
four or five quarts of beer each time the men came back
with a new load. They would eat sporadically during the
day, never stopping for more than a bit of provender
carried back and forth from house to barn as they
returned with loads.

As they pulled out for another trip into the fields, I
made more ice, washed the dishes, wedged laundry—
the sweat-soaked and hay-pierced clothes they had
changed from—into the machine, hoping earnestly that
at least one load would get dry before they would need
to change again. Soon I would have to plan toward the
fried chicken, potatoes, and pies we would eat that night
when my husband, too weary to lift any more, called
quitting time. At midnight, I would still be in my
kitchen, still be cleaning up, still be making ice against
Sunday's needs.

But Sunday was easier. The men were tired; their pace
had slowed, the loft was full, and the hay had only to be

set in place on the ground-level corridors of the barn. It was not quite as hot that day, and muscles that were tight and screaming yesterday had loosened to work a bit more. By midmorning the trucks had pulled out for the second load of the day, and I had started the first load of overalls. I slipped out to the garden, leaving Rebecca still asleep. I was alone for the first time in thirty-six hours.

On this day in 1226, in the time of God's year that he most loved, the Little Frenchman of Assisi finally slipped over into the reality he had always known was on the other side of all this. I thought of him as I walked toward the garden. The luxury of the silent fields stretched unbroken around me from the orchard to the cemetery beyond the close. Only the grasshoppers and my thoughts were at work in the dry, brown fullness of the fall harvest. I moved, bucket in hand, among the red peppers. They stood like Caesar bleeding from his wounds, the long slashes of red dripping into my bucket as my fingers pinched them easily from the stems. The eggplants, pendulous as the flesh of old men, settled softly into my palms as I raised them from the low vines where they hung, globular and purple, under camouflaging leaves. They went gently into the bucket, beautiful and asymmetrical in their absurd heaviness.

The okra I always saved until last. Here in the rows of this most sensual of plants, I passed back and forth letting the tiny fur prick my arms and hands until my skin grew red and angry from the constant rub of our contact. The stalks snapped and bled their milk as I gathered the thrusting pods and then yanked from below the wound the leaf that had borne the pod in its upward thrust. The okra was servile in its need to be hurt, and only in its bleeding would it come to bear again for me. I bruised it with understanding as I moved across the rows, harvesting and pulling.

The sun was warm and clear, but already I could feel the weakness of its light, the growing distance between us and it. The tepeed beans were bloomless, barren vines now sending only tendrils out for sustenance and water. Grief-stricken, I felt the need to lie down, to rest briefly in the valley between their rows, to let the tendrils crawl across me until they covered me and we sank together into the dying autumn. Like a mournful child, I needed to crunch the dry soil into dust and smear my body until I, too, was earth; until I, too, could end with what I had loved. The attraction to the dust moved in my fingers, and I gathered it into my hands, to crumble it across my sandaled feet, to begin my own burial.

But the trucks were coming. Lumbering and hot, they crossed over the pasture terraces, over the ditches, and moved toward the barn. The men were hallowing for beer, water, and tea. I picked up my buckets and moved back toward the kitchen, the dry mud still caught in my shoes and on my feet. Not yet, my Francis, not yet.

CHAPTER 11

In Sickness and in Health

There is no way for me to speak objectively of St. Luke or of his feast day. I live with a physician, have spent almost 75 percent of my life with him, and plan to spend 100 percent of its remainder with him. That fact alone means that the patron saint of healing will always be seen by all of us in this household in terms of medicine's most immediate and visible practitioner. It means that inevitably we see St. Luke in terms of the characteristics of personality and of mental function that we know from experience draw a person into the role of physician and that also make him or her able in it.

Even if all of the above were not part of my experience, however, I would probably still have some trouble being casual about St. Luke. Most of us do. Because he was a physician and because of those very characteristics and turns of disposition that mark his profession, he was in many ways the dominant Gospel writer. Of the many parables of our Lord recorded in the New Testament, eighteen of them are related to us only by St. Luke. Without his educated and curious ear, in other words, more than half of our Lord's active teachings would have gone untransmitted. Likewise, six of the Lord's miracles are recorded only by Luke, five of them quite naturally dealing with healing itself. My three favorite miracles as a child were, in fact, peculiar to St. Luke: The draught of fishes, the crooked woman made straight, and the raising for the widow of Nain of her son.

We cannot leave Luke, though, without recalling what must be the most poignant words in the Epistles. Paul, approaching death and under house arrest in Rome, writes for the last time to the young Timothy. In closing the letter of farewell, he adds, "Only Luke is with me" (2 Timothy 4:11). Of course he was; he was a physician. And, from living with a physician, I know whose burden it is to stand by, not only in life but even into death. . . .

In the beginning, the calf's name was Velvet. She was simply "the sick one" by the time it was all over.

Yet even in the beginning Velvet did not quite fit her. She was not black, but russet, with a white star on her forehead and a white blaze on her left front leg. Her softness, like that of all calves, was the coarse-textured softness of the well locked and well tended, not of the supple and silky. Nonetheless, Velvet it was . . . originally.

She was born on one of those fiercely windy days that mark the deep winter weeks of west Tennessee. The sky never got brighter than twilight that day, and the ice flakes blew, like falling leaves in autumn, off the twigs and limbs of the trees in the close. Dolly was her mother and a good breeder. She had brought herself in early that morning, first to the feedlot and then into the open corridor of the barn itself. There was no trouble in persuading her to move into the hay-strewn stall that Sam had prepared for her, and no protest when John shut the door on her. Before suppertime, we had Velvet.

By the spring, Velvet was as strong and friendly and fleshed-out as all Dolly's calves had been, just a bit more adventuresome. Occasionally, looking at our own rambunctious Rebecca, Sam and I would laugh about Velvet and reassure each other that the more offspring one has, the more daring they become; but we never meant for our joke to be taken seriously.

Then came the rains of April. Velvet had trouble bending her personality to her environment. All the places that a calf could cavort in or graze on or even just be curious about were muddy at first, then slippery, then miry. Life in the lower pasture was not good. It certainly was not sure-footed. And that was how it happened.

Between our pond and the first fields of the untended land behind us, there is a dam that Sam threw up years ago in order to raise the water level in the pond. The structure, put there through days of excruciating labor with tractor, blade, truck, and sheer determination, always stands at least three feet above water level even in the rainy season, and at least six to seven feet above the fence and the empty field below it.

The path across the dam, worn down originally by the children playing on it, fishing from it, and racing across it, is no more than two feet at its widest point. But cows are as gullible and as lazy as any other of God's creatures and so, though not sure-footed as a species in the first place, before long they began to follow the children across the dam. They apparently came to regard the narrow path as a timesaving bridge that prevented their having to go around the pond to get to the upper meadow and Mary's Hill. Since cows seem to have nothing but time, it always amused me to watch them line up single file to begin their trek across the dam, its narrowness clearly causing them concern, but the attraction of its shortcut proving to be irresistible.

It was not, then, that Velvet was where her mother would not have wanted her to be on the day she fell. It was simply that Velvet was crossing in a manner neither her mother nor her other kin would have approved of, had they known. I saw it happen, in fact. I was standing at the kitchen window daydreaming about how lovely it was to be dry instead of out in the drizzle and to be female instead of Sam, who, at that moment, propped against the doorjamb, was struggling into his boots so he could go do his evening chores.

The minute Sam finally got into those boots and opened the back door, of course, every cow on the place knew it; and long before I heard him clang the chain on the orchard gate, every one of them already knew he was going to clang it. Slowly, as I watched from my warm, dry kitchen, they started that bovine shuffle with which cows always reassemble themselves. Once again turned into a herd, they moved together toward the barn and food—all except Velvet. She was intensely involved with something at the edge of the pond. Dolly was almost out of her sight when Velvet looked up and saw the departing herd. It was then that she tried the impossible. She tried to gambol across the dam. She made it about four feet across before her feet went. I saw her legs slide under her, watched her roll onto her flanks, and then chuckled as the whole of her, mud and all, fell off the far side of the dam.

It was when Velvet did not immediately come back up into view that it occurred to me that she might be hurt. I waited a few minutes and, when nothing happened, put on my boots. By the time I had got as far as the pasture fence, I could see Velvet climbing back up onto the dam. As I watched, she slowly made her way across and up the hill toward the barn. I went back into the house, took off my boots, and finished getting supper on the table, giving no further thought to Velvet.

When Sam came in, he was laughing. "What did that dumb calf do? Fall into the pond?"

I told him of Velvet's attempt to be a colt instead of a calf.

"Well, she's the muddiest thing I ever saw! I got most of it off, but Dolly and the grass are going to have to do the rest."

"Did it hurt her?"

"No, doesn't look like it. Seems to have hit something, probably one of the fence posts, with her right side, but it just roughed up her hide . . . didn't even break the skin." And we sat down to eat, having no more concern than a good tale to share with the children as they came to the table.

It was at least a month later—the weather had already grown warmer, and Sam and the boys were no longer throwing out extra hay for the animals every night—that Rebecca remarked that Velvet sure did look funny. The only reason I remember it is that Sam went out after supper that night just to check and said, rather casually to me later, "Becca's right. That calf does look funny, sort of malnourished, in fact. But Dolly's got plenty of milk. We'd better watch her for a day or two."

His day or two was to stretch into five months of watching. At first, Velvet was merely weak. She, who had always run and played and nipped, now lay most of the day beside her mother. She no longer came to the fence when Rebecca was in the hammock or to the gate with the herd when Rebecca was in the orchard picking faulty apples and pears for them. It was in those weeks of late June and early July that she ceased to be Velvet and became the sick one. It was a removal, a distancing, that the children created by themselves.

In the course of his years as a physician, Sam has talked, from time to time, of the anguish peculiar to treating the terminally ill. The dying endure a specific form of suffering, not because of their illness or their coming death or even their often intractable pain, but because of their isolation. They experience the withdrawal from them of everyone—their families first, then their acquaintances and, near the end, sometimes even of their medical support teams. Probably no part of medicine has been more in Sam's conversation than this one thing: his frustration that it should happen; his anger that time and time again he should have to watch that withdrawal from someone for whom he cared; his rage that he himself should still feel so strongly the animal instinct to withdraw and should, after all these years, still have to fight against himself in order to stay the course. Now here we were watching the same thing in our children. No one had said that the sick one would die; it was built into the changing of her name. They had loved on and handled Velvet; they only watched the sick one.

By July, Sam knew what had happened. "The blow to her side when she fell off the dam. It must have caused a stricture."

"She's starving?"

"She starving . . . not enough getting through the narrowing in her gut where she hit it . . . certainly not enough to keep her alive for much longer this way." And he began to mix various kinds of high-protein formulas and pabulums for her. Most of his efforts only came back up again, frequently all over him as well as the calf.

Then the bloating began. In her hunger she continued to eat, and the food, unable to pass out of her stomach, stayed there. Over the weeks of August and September, her front grew more and more distended and her midsection more and more emaciated. Old Buck Jones, the vet we had used for years, just simply wouldn't come anymore.

"It's no use, Doc. You ain't gonna save this one regardless of how many times you call me out here" had been his parting shot the last time he came to see her in mid-September.

But Sam continued his ministrations, carrying the nursing bottle to the barn two times a day, sometimes three. Then Velvet rallied. She began to move around more during the day. I even saw her playing one afternoon with another calf. The distension went down a bit, and if her middle did not get fatter, it at least did not get bonier. The children and I were encouraged. Only Sam shook his head. "She's just quit eating all together, is all," he said. "And the decreased pressure in her belly makes her feel better."

By mid-October it was obvious that he had been right. For two days she huddled in the barn, lying all day on the hay in the stall where she had been born. Dolly no longer even came around her or showed any interest at all in her whereabouts, nor did the children. Finally on Sunday afternoon after lunch, Sam came back in from seeing about her in the barn. Saying nothing, he moved around the kitchen packing his pockets with string and matches and even my baster. "Will you help me?" he asked as he crossed behind me and got the big butcher knife out of the kitchen drawer, adding it to his jacket full of supplies. I nodded yes as I dried my hands on the dishtowel. "Come on when you finish then," and he was gone out the door.

The children were all doing homework, and I was certain that I did not want their help, so I said nothing as I slipped quietly out the back door and followed him to the barn. By the time I got there he had already taken one of the wide rolls of black plastic he uses for tarping and spread it across the stall floor and over the hay. He was lifting the calf onto the center of it as I came in. She was toxic by this time and unconscious, a dead weight in his arms. The exertion of positioning her was already making trickles of sweat down Sam's neck as I knelt down to help him cover her with the old blankets he had brought from the house.

"Not much of an operating room, is it?" He laughed at me sardonically.

"Not much." Even as I answered him, all the years we had shared together so long ago when he had been fresh out of school and in general practice in the country came running back. It had been primitive then, too, those years before residency and fellowship and subspecialty, before fancy hospitals and elaborate drugs and elegant equipment; those years as doctor in a mill village among the incredibly poor with only his inventiveness between us and their deaths. I had helped because I had had to. He had taught me, often right on the spot, and I had loved the learning and the being together. Sometimes we had lost, but most of the time we had won.

But this time we were going to lose. I knew enough medicine to know that. Listening to his labored breathing as he adjusted her one last time, I said it. "Why? Why are we doing this now?"

"Last week it would have killed her. There's no way on God's earth to anesthetize her, you know that. This week she's too near gone to even know we're here, much less what we're doing."

"But you can't possibly get a sterile field out here in all this mess?"

"You noticed that, did you?" His sarcasm was again more sardonic than biting, his mind too much involved in his own efforts to be concerned with mine. "But I'll tell you one thing. If she makes it till I can get in there and there's any way in the world to reconnect that gut around the stricture, we're sure going to give it the royal try, and the devil can take the hindmost!" Just as in the old days, I had just been given my instructions, or as much of them as there was ever going to be.

He straightened out her legs to expose the injured side. Rising, he went out and came back again with three of his clamp lights. He hung them from the tack racks and ran an extension cord to each. Still not enough light to really see. He left me with the calf again. In the corner beyond her he had already laid out the sutures and clamps and sponges that, in all our years in the country, he had always kept in the shop cabinet against some emergency, some injury to children or neighbor or self.

He came back into the corridor, and I heard him rummaging in the tool chest. Coming into the stall, he handed me his portable spotlight. "You'll have to hold it" was all he said before he dropped to his knees again between the calf's extended legs and began to palpate her abdomen. She didn't even stir as his hands moved back and forth, feeling and defining as they went. Never once did she appear to know that we were there, even when he pressed hard over the upper part of her gut.

"Here it is," he said. "Turn on the light."

And I did as he picked up the knife and opened the skin deftly and swiftly. Then, more slowly and more deliberately, watching her for any sign of stress as he cut, he moved through the muscle and fascia, clamping the bleeders as he went, and laid open her abdominal cavity. There exposed in clear view were the stomach and the intestines; and between them, just where the stomach empties into the digestive tract, was the stricture, the six or seven inches of dead intestine. He lifted it up, felt it between his fingers, and shook his head.

"Want to try?" I said.

"Can't. Gut's already gone below it."

Looking beyond his hand, I saw the rest of the intestine purple and engorged beyond the spotlight's peripheral glow.

"Damn it all!" The sweat, even in the cold barn, was running down his neck, and his hair was wet from the exertion of opening her and from, I thought, his own intensity.

I watched him as he settled down on the black plastic. Impervious to the feces and blood around him, he began to clean off her skin. "Go get the gun."

I did not say anything, just turned off the spotlight, hung it on a hook, took one last look at him there between the calf's legs and covered in her waste, and left. I had not gone as far as the orchard gate when I heard the first blow. I also heard the crack as her skull gave way beneath it. There were two more rapid blows and then silence. Standing there with one hand on the gate and listening to the quiet, I remembered that he had rummaged in his toolbox before we began—and that he had had the hammer as well as the spotlight when he had come back into the stall. He had never intended to make her wait for the gun.

I turned and went back to the barn. In the stall he was covering her with the black tarping. The hammer lay near the door where he had thrown it. He looked up startled, still on his knees and his hands still grasping the corners of the plastic, as I came in. "I didn't mean for you to come back so soon . . ." His voice trailed off.

"I'll help you clean up."

"No," he said, still on the floor and still working to secure the corners of the tarp over her. "No. I want the children to do that."

"All three of them?" My heart rose to Rebecca's pain in seeing this scene, in having to carry supplies and help clean tools.

He got up, slapping his thighs and stomping his feet as he did so. "We tried. We lost, but we did try. And we will also finish it. Don't you want them to learn that from us?"

I nodded because he was right, not because I had the wisdom it took to agree. He touched my arm lightly, looking hard into my eyes. "This is just another part of what they will need to know," he said.

Then, as abruptly as his words, he was gone to call his children.

CHAPTER 12

The Necropolis
at Our House

If angels are pleasant for us to consider in the warm, ripe days of fall, the dead seem somewhat less affable to most of us, especially in the growing bleakness and cold of early November.

The church has always taught the doctrine of the communion of the saints—the principle that there is an unbroken union of all saints, whether in this world or out of it; that that community is inviolate; that it is a communion beyond the reach of mutability. Exactly what is the relationship between the faithful dead and the faithful living has been debated for centuries, but almost no branch of the faith questions the notion that there is a relationship. And almost every branch has been amazingly content to let the believer treat the problem in the way most comfortable to that individual as long as he or she didn't get too outspoken or too definitive in any opinions.

However the individual may wish to deal with the dead and/or the ongoing communion of the saints, the church still holds All Saints' as a major feast day and still demands of us as believers some consideration of the question of death itself and of those who have passed into it.

At the foot of the pasture, just where the fence meets the bog, there is a homemade stile fashioned years ago of stones and logs by little Tickles seeking easier access to the village cemetery beyond our property line. Although it is not beautiful, it has, as contrivances go, been remarkably effective, having carried more than its fair share of cousins, playmates, and siblings across the fence from pasture games to graveyard play. There was a time when even the older children could recite the names and histories of at least three dozen of the cemetary's dead, so great was their intimacy with the place.

They played originally, of course, without any reverence and, as very young children, without any acquired regard for spooks and goblins. The cemetery was simply another part of our part of the village where another set of neighbors existed—statically perhaps, but existed.

It used to fascinate me that the children always spoke of the buried in the present tense.

"The General's got some kind of awful, red gooey stuff growing up his stone. John tried to scrape it off, but it wouldn't come. What do you reckon it is?"

"Miss Pink's flowers are dead. Do you think she'd like some of our marigolds?"

"Sam was cracking walnuts on Mrs. Todd's foot marker, but I told him to stop. She wouldn't like it a bit if she could see the mess he's made!"

And then, as each started to school and began to realize the broadening social world that makes school tolerable for most of us, I was equally fascinated to watch each of them tie their new friends backward, so to speak, to their dead ones.

"I met a new kid today—name's Jimmy Brandon. His granddaddy's over there under that last oak by the corner of the fence."

As the children grew older, they played less raucously in the cemetery, as they did everywhere else, of course. Each briefly went through a Halloween phase of wanting earnestly to believe in scary places and of wanting our cemetery to perform that service for them. But as a thriller, it was a washout. After all their years of playing and daydreaming there, the place was too comfortable, too familiar to make their blood race or their eyes see what was not there. So now it matters almost not at all to any of them except as a storybook matters: loved in childhood but outgrown in adolescence, it still matters, still instructs, still is part of what the adult becomes.

When she was home one autumn for a visit, Laura went down to see about it. At first I didn't know where she had gone until Becca, who knew everything, said, "She's gone to see the General. I saw her climbing over the stile."

When she got back, I was cooking lunch. "How was he?" I asked as she came in.

She grinned, a little sheepishly maybe, but her eyes twinkled as she answered. "Just fine, I think. At least he didn't complain." And then, in typical Laura fashion, she added, "And I did remember to ask him."

Despite such occasional visits, though, so badly built a stile would in the normal course of things have grown grassier and grassier each summer over the years. It would, in the normal course of things, have sunk lower and lower with the rains of each fall until it completely reverted to the rubble and lumber from which it came. But then grandchildren began coming along, still too little to haul logs and rocks or even to shift those that have already been hauled. As a first social experience with the dead, however, the old stile has certainly remained a comfortable one, and for that reason alone, it probably deserves more loyalty from us than most stiles do. At least that's what Sam Sr. said one day when he came back in from restacking it. Actually what he said was, "Why knock a good thing when you've got it?" but I think it means the same thing.

Epilogue

Unlike those who have preceded us, we can now know with our intellects and prove with our theorems that there is no time; we can establish that, at the speed of light, time is not, in other words.

The church knows that same principle by faith; and by their faith our forebears honored it. In effect they gave over half their liturgical observances to honoring it, or rather to honoring the rifts in time that prove its nonexistence—to angels and to saints, to prophecy and to mystery, to the dead who are living.

In a way, like Ordinary Time, the liturgical season it treats of, this has been a book about something that isn't, so that we may more properly know what is . . . a paradox, in other words, within the skin of whose enigma the I-Am waits for us to come home.

No season of the church's calendar and no portion of its liturgy begins with more confusion than does the seventh and last part of the sacred year, those final weeks that stretch from Ascensiontide through to Advent.

Suffice it to say that all Christians seem to agree that the ascension of our Lord took place forty days after his resurrection. We all also seem to hold in common agreement the acceptance of Pentecost. The day of Pentecost—no more than a Greek word lifted directly into our language and meaning "fifty"—comes ten days after Ascension and once lent its name to the whole season in which it falls. Simple so far.

If one thinks about it mathematically, one realizes without even looking at a lectionary or a service book that Ascension must always come on Thursday, since Easter always comes on Sunday. One also calculates very readily the fact that the Sunday after Ascension is still part of the Great Fifty Days of Easter. The following Sunday, however, is the tricky one.

The Sunday after the Sunday after the Ascension is the Day of Pentecost. It plainly and clearly falls fifty days after Easter and fulfills its semantic obligation to be fifty. It is also the day on which the tongues of flame descended on the assembled apostles; the day when the Holy Ghost dramatically entered the church's history by occupying the bodies of the believers; the day when those around the assembled were convicted and converted by what they saw with their eyes and heard with their ears.

In its own way, Pentecost's story is the most compelling one in our faith. Christ is gone, removed, triumphantly absent. Now life—human, humdrum, secular life must end its mourning, hang up its miracles, question its memories. And History would have done all those things—would have helped life to erode its one truth—except for Pentecost. On that day in one singular event, the nature of humanity, or of some among humanity, is publicly reconstituted so as to house the nature of God . . . and History is relegated to being a tool instead of a cause. Strong stuff in anybody's book, and one cannot really blame the church for having treated the results a bit gingerly, to say the least.

Without incarnate God and resurrected Lord, certainly, Pentecost would not have happened. But it is a prudent believer who always knows, twenty-four hours a spiritual day, that were it not for Pentecost, both the Incarnation and the Resurrection would have been unreceivable, would have been remembered longings, as poignant and useless as are our memories of flying during the naps and dreams of infancy.

Pentecost hooked us up to the myth. It put the myth inside and made it fact for the soul. It became, thereby, the Great Miracle; it became also everyone's miracle, the possession of each believer and the most intimate chamber of mystery.

Every religion must have its canon of mysteries, of course. It is something of an idiosyncrasy that all of ours save two—the Incarnation and the Resurrection—are tucked into the twenty-five-odd weeks that begin with Pentecost and end on the first Sunday of Advent with the beginning of the church's new year. This kind of compression of so much observance into half a year's time can be a threat by overexposure to one's sense of wonder, and from time to time that possibility has made the church a bit nervous.

Religion's mysteries, in order to be effective, must not only be observed within a well-ordered calendar, but they must also deal very specifically with reality and variant reality; that is the function of mysteries. Christianity's needs in that regard are the same as those of any other religion from the most primitive animism to the most sophisticated Buddhism.

Many a man or woman would also like to say that because human nature is human nature, the variants of reality that a religion must address will be the same from the most primitive animism to the most sophisticated Buddhism. If it were not for Pentecost, the Christian could agree. Unfortunately, however—at least from the secularist's point of view—the Christian cannot say that, because every Christian knows that Christian human nature was changed at Pentecost.

The result of Pentecost is that now the "god" in us is God looking at God—an exercise that is, at least for those who have passed through their own Pentecost, a little like trying to see into one's own eyes or bite one's own teeth, to use Buddhism's analogy. And that's a hard bill of goods to sell, much less explain.

But perhaps the most comfortable result of all our wrestling with paradox to extract its truth lies in a fairly recent decision by the Roman Catholic Church and some Protestant churches. Very few things have helped all of us more than that decision to call the time from Pentecost to Advent by its current name . . . to call it Ordinary Time.

As a name for a liturgical season—for half the calendar year, in fact—Ordinary Time, too, is stark in its simplicity, for, as we all know, there is no such thing.